Carlisle

History and Guide

Carlisle

History and Guide

Mike McCarthy

ALAN SUTTON

First published in the United Kingdom in 1993 by
Alan Sutton Publishing Ltd
Phoenix Mill · Far Thrupp · Stroud · Gloucestershire

First published in the United States of America in 1993 by
Alan Sutton Publishing Inc · 83 Washington Street · Dover · NH 03820

British Library Cataloguing in Publication Data

A catalogue record for this book is available from the British Library.

Library of Congress Cataloging in Publication Data applied for

Jacket illustration: The Citadel, Carlisle (*Photograph, Syndication International Ltd*)

ISBN 0-7509-0236-1

Typeset in 10/13 Times.
Typesetting and origination by
Alan Sutton Publishing Limited.
Printed in Great Britain by
Redwood Books, Trowbridge, Wiltshire

Contents

CHAPTER ONE

The Romans

Prehistoric Times and the Arrival of the Romans

In the year AD 72 the Romans marched north from their newly established base at York, crossed the Pennines by way of Stainmore and entered Cumbria. Marching up the fertile Eden Valley, they arrived at what we know as Carlisle where they built a fort at the junction of the Rivers Eden and Caldew.

They were not the first to set foot in this area. For centuries, prehistoric man had exploited this undulating landscape with its peat mosses, pockets of good, light, easily tilled soils, and more extensive tracts of heavier land. These early settlers are shadowy figures in a landscape quite different to that of today. Of the many sites discovered through aerial photography, few can be dated and even fewer have been excavated.

It is possible, however, to show that the area was occupied in the Middle Stone Age (Mesolithic). At this remote period, earlier than about 4000 BC, small groups exploited areas around the coasts and rivers, clearing forest and hunting game. Gradually new settlers moved in during the New Stone Age (Neolithic), bringing with them techniques for tilling the soil. A large number of stone axes and other objects have been discovered in north Cumbria and at Carlisle, many made of stone quarried at Great Langdale in the Lake District. As in many other parts of the country it was these early farmers who made the first real impact on the landscape, using their stone axes to clear primeval woodlands for settlement and for agriculture.

In Carlisle itself archaeology has revealed some traces of these distant farmers. Marks made in the underlying glacial soils by primitive ploughs have been found at Blackfriars Street, below Tullie House Museum and in Lowther Street. This early farming activity is thought to date to the Neolithic, partly on the basis of stone tools, including axes, which have been found.

Linear grooves made by New Stone Age (Neolithic) ploughs at Blackfriars Street

How long this activity lasted is not known, but from around 2000 BC, during the Bronze Age, the climate began to get progressively wetter, and conditions were made worse from around 750 BC when the weather grew colder. Meteorologists who study the evidence for weather in ancient times have suggested that there were periods of prolonged stormy westerly winds which particularly affected western Britain during the late Bronze Age and Iron Age. Such conditions could have led to changes in the pattern of early settlements and in the methods of farming, especially on heavier soils. In Carlisle the soils are known to have undergone periodic waterlogging in ancient times, and it is suggested that the deteriorating climate could have led to the early farmers abandoning the land here in favour of other places. There have been few finds of this early period in the city centre, although a barbed and tanged arrowhead and a round-house, which may be Bronze Age or Iron Age, were unearthed in The Lanes. Outside the city centre, a few burials and other objects have been discovered at various places including Aglionby, Rickerby and Garlands.

In late prehistoric times up to the arrival of the Romans, there is ample evidence from various sources about the predominantly wooded nature of the locality. There was much alder woodland, with some willow, on the wetter lands in the valleys of the Eden, Caldew and Petteril. On the higher ground and the slopes above the river valleys, and doubtless on the heavier, less easily worked boulder clays, were deciduous forests with oak, elm, ash and hazel. There may have been some variety in these woodlands, ranging from relatively dense canopies formed by trees that began life in the second and third centuries BC, to more open woods and scrubland. Within this landscape we can picture small farming communities living in the typical round-houses of the period, surrounded by cleared areas of fields and pasture. We know little of the economic basis of these societies as yet, although it is likely that cattle, sheep and pigs were important elements. Unlike southern Britain, which in late prehistoric times has been termed an agroscape in which the whole landscape was intensively farmed, in north Cumbria settlement may have been much less dense and society less hierarchical. At present the available evidence points to the Romans as the first to establish nucleated settlements in this area, one of the first being at Carlisle.

This took place as a result of the Romans' need to establish firm control over the great northern tribal confederacy known as the Brigantes, and who had risen in revolt in the year AD 69. The Roman soldiers set up their fort, defended by a rampart of turf and timber, in the winter of AD 72–3 under the leadership of the governor of Britain, Petillius Cerialis, who was also the son-in-law of the Emperor Vespasian. Attached to the southern side of the fort was a small defended annexe. Such close dating is rarely possible in archaeology, but in this instance analysis of the tree-rings on some of the timbers provides us with precise evidence.

The fort at Carlisle, far from being an isolated outpost, was part of a network of forts linked by road to many places in northern Britain. It follows that the fortunes of Carlisle were also tied into events taking place elsewhere. At present, despite the enormous amount of work that has been expended on researching aspects of the Roman military conquest, and the analyses of the scattered historical sources, our understanding of these events is still very limited.

Initially the garrison here may have consisted of an infantry cohort, but other units are also known, including a detachment of legionaries of the Twentieth Legion who probably arrived late in AD 83 hotfoot from the decisive battle of Mons Graupius in Scotland. Written evidence they left behind tells us that two of these legionaries

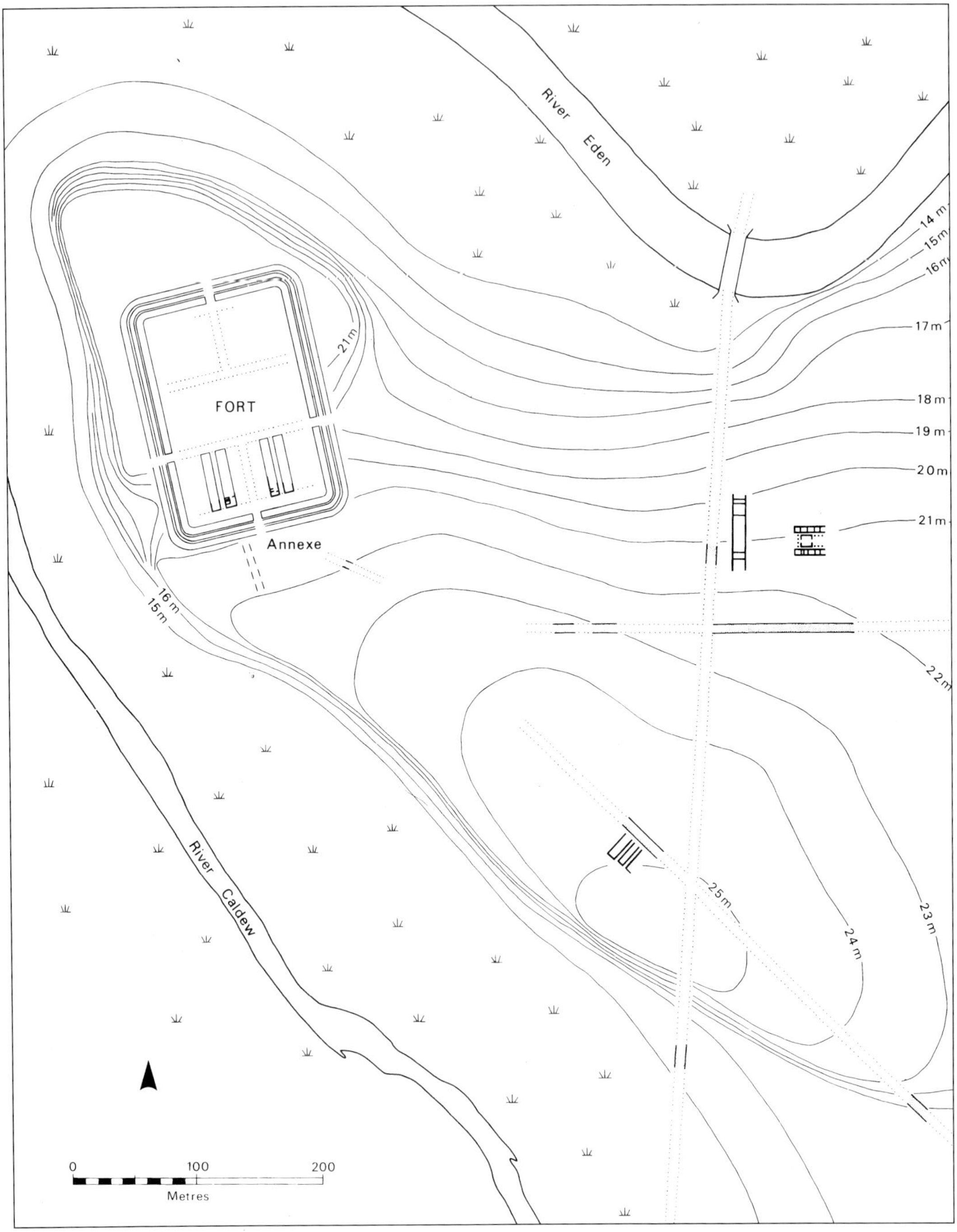
River Eden
FORT
21m
Annexe
16m
15m
14m
15m
16m
17m
18m
19m
20m
21m
22m
23m
24m
25m
River Caldew
0
100
200
Metres

General view of the Roman fort at Annetwell Street. On the right is the cobbled road, and the dark lines and dots in the centre and left are the foundations of barracks and other structures

entered into an agreement whereby one lent the other 100 *denarii*, perhaps three months pay, in November 83. It seems that for the first thirty years or so of its life, the fort may have at times accommodated a composite garrison with troops drawn from more than one regiment. Among them were cavalrymen who have left evidence of their presence in the form of horse gear and animal fodder. Even intestinal parasites that live in the guts of horses have been found.

Writing tablets also tell us that by this time Carlisle was already known to the Romans as *Luguvalium*. Letters were addressed to one Marcus Iulius Martialis, thought by the letter writer to have been based at either Newstead, near Melrose in Scotland, or Carlisle. Another letter was sent to a man named Domitius Tertius who is described by a word difficult to interpret but which meant either a dealer in cereals or a worker in gold.

A map of Roman Carlisle in the late first century showing the position of the fort and annexe, roads and other buildings excavated to date

During the late 80s and 90s the Romans gradually withdrew their forces from Scotland in a series of stages. This process would have led to the concentration of forces further south and must have had an impact on such places as Carlisle and Corbridge, both occupying key

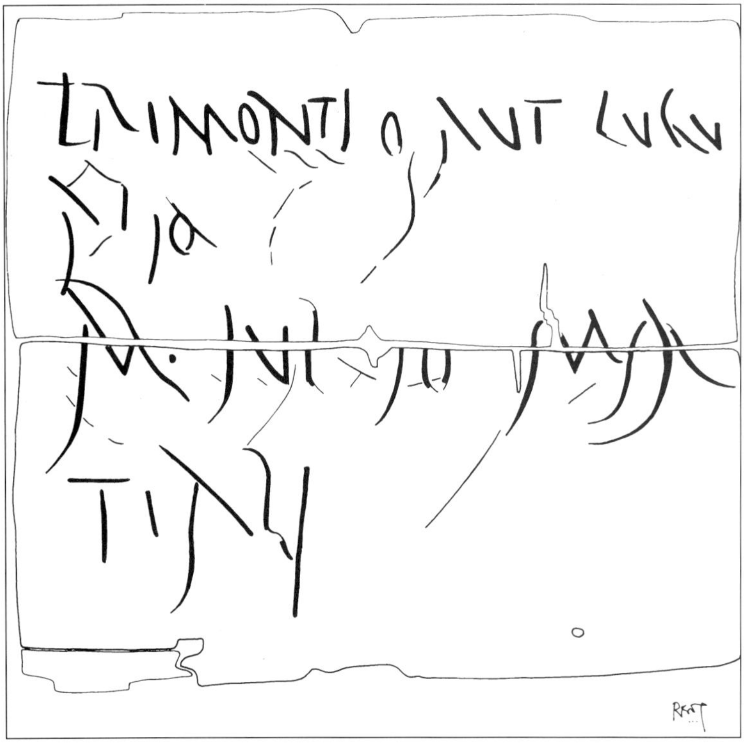

Writing tablet from the fort annexe at Castle Street bearing the inscription '*Trimontio aut Luguvalio Marco Iulio Martiali*': at *Trimontium* (Newstead) or *Luguvalium* (Carlisle); to Marcus Iulius Martialis. *Luguvalium* is a pre-Roman place-name derived from the important Celtic deity, Lug

Writing tablet bearing the inscription '*Kimio Sedato*', to Kimius Sedatus, part of an address, found in the fort annexe at Castle Street

The side of a wooden cage found slumped into the fill of the annexe ditch found below Tullie House Museum

strategic positions on the main roads on the eastern and western sides of the country. When the detachment of legionaries arrived in Carlisle in AD 83, it resulted in the demolition of the existing barracks and the erection of new, more capacious buildings.

The withdrawal from Scotland may also have meant that very senior Roman officials were temporarily based here. In The Lanes, two impressive buildings dating to the 80s or 90s have been discovered. One of them was of massive construction, with plastered walls and incorporating a central heating system (hypocaust). Nearby was a smaller building with three ranges of rooms and a fourth side entered through a portico. This building resembles a temple in plan but the truth is that the precise function of both buildings is not certain. The buildings had a short life, perhaps only a decade or less, before they were deliberately demolished and their burnt remains, including spreads of charcoal, mortar and molten lead, littered the site.

The withdrawal from Scotland may have had a further impact on Carlisle, initiating a new wave of building construction, for at three different sites it is possible to identify timbers all felled at more or less the same time, in the years AD 92–4. This coincidence of dates strongly argues for widespread changes taking place. Within the fort modifications were made to the ramparts and other buildings, and the land within the annexe was completely reorganized. At about this time buildings, thought to be domestic houses, were being built at what we know as Blackfriars Street. Here, timber-built structures divided into several rooms, and with floors of clay and earth, seem to have been closely spaced along the main road to the south.

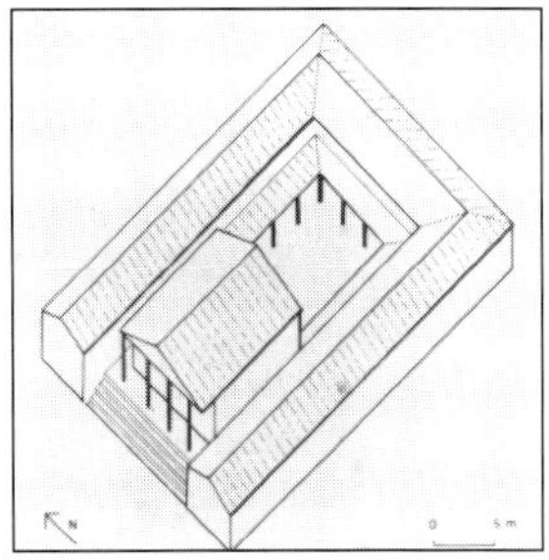

A reconstruction of a possible temple discovered in The Lanes

Unlike Blackfriars Street, the land at The Lanes, on the eastern side of the Roman settlement, was not densely occupied. The buildings including the temple-like structure, formerly occupied by senior officials, were swept away and the land laid out as relatively large enclosures, bounded by a mixture of fences, tree windbreaks, hedges and gulleys. Buildings within the enclosures almost certainly accommodated cattle and perhaps sheep, as well as people. The remains of the cattle show that many were of the 'Celtic shorthorn' variety, and were mature to elderly when slaughtered. They were probably kept for dairying and for draught purposes. These bones contrast with those excavated at the fort site that represent cattle slaughtered for their meat.

The population probably included a civilian element, even though the military must have exerted considerable control over the shape and nature of the burgeoning settlement. At present, although there is no means of telling who lived here, or where they came from, it is possible to speculate and suggest that some may have come from further south following the army, while others were of local extraction. Doubtless the presence of the army as a potential market acted as a magnet for local traders and farmers.

In these early years the requirements of the army, and the ability of the civilians to keep it supplied, must have been of paramount concern. To some extent one could envisage the civilian zone as resembling an extra-mural annexe to the fort. Small-scale manufacture and repair, perhaps with some shops or booths along the street frontage, and farming, must have figured prominently. At Blackfriars Street, the plans of the buildings, together with their contents, betoken the domestic life of a population able to afford not just the standard knick-knacks of Roman life – brooches, toilet implements, glass beads, glossy red samian pottery and the like – but also polychrome and monochrome glass bowls as well as clear glass cups, flasks and jugs. These relatively expensive wares, together, presumably, with the imported wine and other foodstuffs to go with them, do not look like the property of an oppressed local farming community. It is conceivable that some of these buildings were occupied by retired soldiers.

Roman timber buildings erected in the fort annexe in the year AD 92–3, Castle Street

The food consumed by the army and other inhabitants of Carlisle was probably obtained from both local and more distant sources. Wheat, for example, may have been imported from elsewhere in the north where the growing season was longer and the climate less damp. Barley, for both malting and animal feed, and meat from cattle, sheep and pigs may have been locally obtained. It is possible to speculate and suggest that the ancient field systems discovered between Stanwix and Tarraby, and the Romano-British settlement unearthed further west at the Infirmary, both had their origins in the first generation of Roman settlement. The growth of native agricultural settlements in the immediate environs of Carlisle may be viewed as a response to the needs of the Roman army's food requirement.

The Growth of Roman Carlisle

The strongly military nature of the settlement of *Luguvalium* was maintained for some time during the second century AD. Throughout the period up to AD 330–40, the fort at Annetwell Street continued to be used. The defences were rebuilt further south on at least two occasions, so that ultimately much of the area formerly occupied by the annexe came to lie within the fort itself. Whereas the rampart defending the first-century fort was made of turf and timber, the later defences were made of clay with a turf revetment and, moreover, they survived to their full height, 1.2–1.5 m. The wall walk was gravel. Within the forts lay the metalled roads, and the stone foundations of barracks.

A reconstruction of the south gate of the Roman fort viewed from the outside. Note that the right-hand door has been nailed up with planks

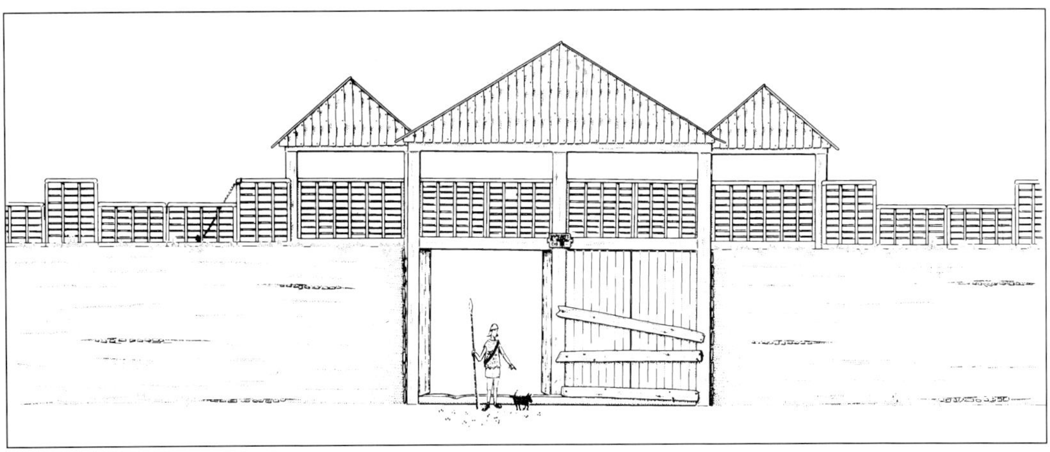

Only a small portion of the fort has been excavated so the line of the northern rampart is not known for certain, but it is possible that the changes to the southern defences imply an increase in fort size, rather than simply indicating a gradual move south. This may therefore also indicate an increase both in the importance and in the size of its garrison.

The area formerly used as an annexe to the early forts may have continued to function in this way for a time after AD 105. A large timber building resting on massive sill beams was constructed. Some of the rooms seem to have been used for storing hay, while at least one contained an oven. An adjacent building, of entirely different construction, was used for storing animal fodder.

The new arrangements in both fort and annexe may be a response to the first stages in formalizing the limits of the empire. First the Emperor Trajan established a frontier, conventionally known as the Stanegate, between the River Tyne and the Solway, and then from AD 122 the Emperor Hadrian consolidated his predecessor's work with the building of a wall from sea to sea. Carlisle thus became a frontier settlement, a role it has continued to perform on and off ever since.

Apart from the rebuilding of the fort and annexe under Trajan, knowledge of the Stanegate frontier in the region of Carlisle is almost non-existent, although recent work by Professor Barri Jones has led to the recognition of a series of watch towers, set within small ditched and embanked enclosures, at Burgh by Sands and further west. Nothing comparable has so far been found in Carlisle.

The line Hadrian's Wall took is a little more certain. Initially built of turf in the west, the Wall ran to the north of the River Eden until it reached a point close to Carlisle Castle and the present cricket ground. At this point it crossed the river and continued westwards on its southern bank. Shortly after Hadrian's Wall was built, forts were added as an additional means of defence. One was built at Stanwix, now a suburb of Carlisle, directly opposite *Luguvalium* on the north bank of the Eden. This fort, usually known as *Petriana* after the regiment known to have been stationed here, was one of the largest on Hadrian's Wall. For a time it housed the crack 1,000-strong cavalry regiment, the *Ala Petriana*, one of the most senior in Britain. For these reasons the site has long fascinated scholars.

The defences of the Hadrian's Wall fort at Stanwix have been located on all four sides, most recently in 1984 when the north wall (with an interval tower) and the north ditch were excavated behind the Cumbria Park Hotel. These finds showed that the fort was enlarged to 9.7 acres in the later second century. Fragments of some internal

Excavations at the Cumbria Park Hotel, Stanwix, revealed the north wall and turret of the Hadrian's Wall fort

buildings are also known, specifically a granary, while a number of other finds have come from the areas to the east and west of the fort, indicating the existence of extra-mural settlements. From the reign of Hadrian, if not a little earlier, not only were there two garrisons on either side of the river within sight of each other, but there were probably two extra-mural populations as well.

At Blackfriars Street, the buildings thought to have been used by retired soldiers in the late first and early second century seem to have been abandoned. The site was left vacant for a short time, long enough for vegetation including some shrubs to grow, before new buildings were erected. This hiatus probably took place *c.* AD 120–30 at the time Hadrian's Wall was being built, but whether or not it was in some way a consequence of the Wall building programme is impossible to say. The new buildings have a number of characteristics that suggest development of a storage/warehousing function. It is easy to imagine that there may well have been a need for storage buildings, perhaps for grain requisitioned by the army from local farmers, outside the fort and annexe.

As the fort in Carlisle continued to exist, despite the proximity of Hadrian's Wall and the fort at Stanwix, it is reasonable to assume that the settlement of *Luguvalium* may have developed further. Did Carlisle become a greater magnet than before, attracting people who benefited by the presence of the soldiers in a variety of ways, as well as performing a market function for local goods and those brought in from a greater distance? If this was the case, we might expect to see infill development along and behind the main street frontages, the creation of new roads and lanes, and tangible signs of Romano-British life in the form of coins, pottery, glass- and metalware, and possibly even evidence of civic pride.

This seems to be what happened, although the stages by which the settlement developed are still uncertain. At Abbey Street, close to the cathedral gatehouse, mortared stone walls belonging to a very large building have been seen during the renewal of sewer trenches. This building occupies part of the site of the former annexe and is thought to be associated with the stone-lined pit, or so-called 'shrine', discovered in the grounds of Tullie House Museum in the 1950s. The walls are sufficiently large as to suggest that it was a public building, and it is tentatively identified as the forum, an important civic building in Roman towns. Whether or not this is correct, fragments of sculpture, such as a large composite capital found in the nineteenth century, must have come from such a building.

Other important remains lie below the floor of the Market Hall. During the reconstruction work carried out in 1990 traces of a large Roman bath-house were discovered near the junction of two Roman roads, one of which was probably the Roman predecessor of Scotch Street. The heated rooms include a hot room (*caldarium*), a possible warm room (*tepidarium*), as well as a cold plunge bath (*frigidarium*) and other rooms besides. As the complete plan of this building was

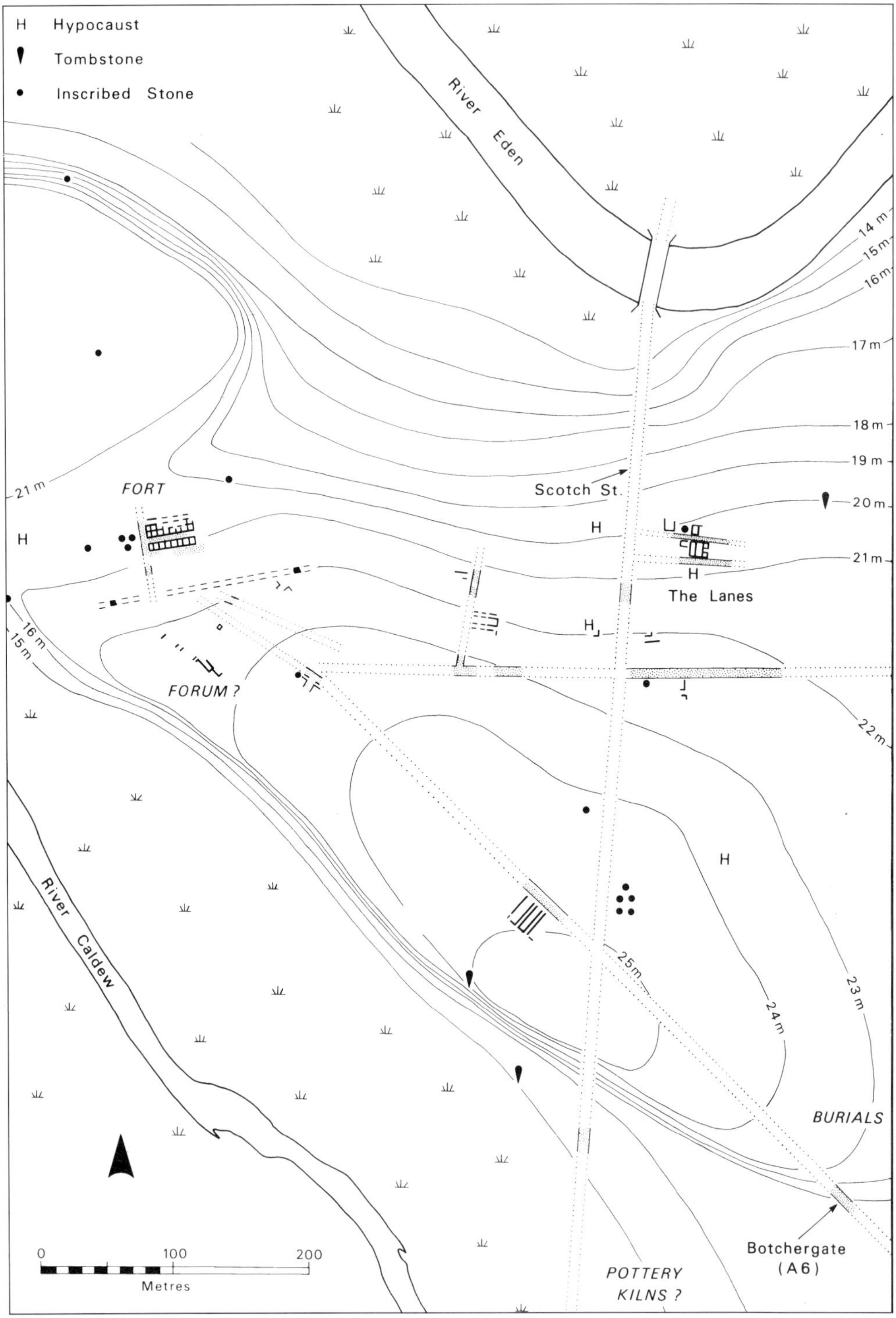
H Hypocaust
Tombstone
Inscribed Stone
River Eden
14 m
15 m
16 m
17 m
18 m
19 m
20 m
21 m
22 m
23 m
24 m
25 m
21 m
16 m
15 m
FORT
H
Scotch St.
H
H
The Lanes
H
FORUM ?
H
River Caldew
BURIALS
Botchergate
(A6)
POTTERY
KILNS ?
0
100
200
Metres

General view of excavations in progress, The Lanes. The features shown here are the badly robbed remains of a stone house

not recovered, there is some uncertainty as to what the bath suite belonged to. One idea is that it was a part of a *mansio*, or hotel for travellers.

On the opposite side of Scotch Street, in what was Keay's Lane, was another stone building. This house began life as a simple rectangular structure but was gradually enlarged in a piecemeal fashion, ending up with a ground plan not dissimilar to that of a Roman villa, and with an underfloor central heating system (*hypocaust*) in one room. It was set back some distance from the main street frontage, and had cobbled yards, a stone-lined well and an ancillary building in front, and open areas to the rear. On its southern side was a narrow cobbled lane beyond which was an open area with a tree; perhaps this was a garden. To the north was another narrow cobbled lane, with what may be a separate property, this time built of timber, lying beyond.

Further up Scotch Street, next to the former Lewthwaite's Lane, there was a building apparently ranged round a courtyard. This, too, is thought to have been a house. The normal type of building, however, was the 'strip' house. This was basically rectangular in plan and was subdivided in a variety of ways into individual rooms.

Map of Roman Carlisle at about AD 200, showing the fort, roads and other buildings excavated to date

A stone-lined well discovered in The Lanes

'Strip' houses were found at Blackfriars Street, where they replaced the buildings referred to earlier as having a storage/warehousing function, at some date late in the second century. Others were recorded at St Mary's Gate before the Cumberland Building Society was rebuilt in 1978–9, and they are the standard building type in the civilian settlements outside Roman forts in the rural areas.

Many of these 'strip' houses may have performed a variety of functions. One of the buildings at Blackfriars Street, for example, contained a large double-flued oven at the rear, and the interior contained substantial spreads of charcoal. Unfortunately no evidence has survived to tell us what the ovens were used for, but it seems likely that the buildings may have been occupied by artisans engaged in the repair and manufacture of equipment and the supply of other goods both to the military and to the native population.

While some of the more important buildings in Carlisle, such as the possible forum and the *mansio*, were of stone, the majority of buildings in *Luguvalium* seem to have had wooden walls based on clay and cobble footings. The walls were doubtless coated in mud, or daub, and whitewashed or plastered, while the floors were simply made of earth, clay or, as at Blackfriars Street, wooden floorboards nailed to joists. None of the elaborate floors often associated with Roman dwellings, such as mosaic pavements, have been found, but the discovery of window glass shows that some buildings at least had glazed windows.

A Roman barrel-lined pit containing an almost complete, but broken, cartwheel

Roofing materials probably included ceramic tiles, perhaps derived from military suppliers or redundant military buildings, but these occur infrequently within the civilian areas of the town, which suggests that they were not in regular use. Wooden shingles and heather and turf were probably used more often. Heather would have been imported from a few miles distant, as it does not occur in the immediate environs of Carlisle. Its presence in archaeological deposits has been taken to imply its use as either animal bedding or roofing material. Similarly, deposits of peat and turves identified at The Lanes, and outside the buildings at Blackfriars Street, may be the result of slippage from a roof.

From what we have seen, then, and from the numerous artefacts discovered in the past hundred years or so, there is ample evidence to suggest that Roman Carlisle enjoyed a measure of growth and prosperity during the second and third centuries AD. Much of this affluence was probably due to the presence of the military. There were, in effect, two settlements here. There were two garrisons, one in Carlisle and one in Stanwix, and each seems to have had its civilian community. Quite what the relationship was between these two important settlements is not known, but their proximity emphasizes the importance of this area to the Romans. It is not unlike the situation at Corbridge in Northumberland, where during the second century military activity is attested in the town south of the Wall at Haltonchesters.

There is a case for both Carlisle and Corbridge performing a wider role in the community. The evidence from Corbridge is not clear cut,

A stone capital from a monumental building

but it could have been an administrative centre, or *civitas* capital, for one of the Brigantian tribes known as the Corieltauvi. Carlisle almost certainly lay within the territory of another Brigantian tribe known as the Carvetii, whose name is recorded on inscriptions. The extent of Carvetian territory is far from clear, but the limited evidence available to us suggests that it lay in eastern Cumbria, with the fertile Eden Valley as the tribe's principal homeland. By the mid-third century the Carvetii had acquired its own administrative centre or *civitas* capital, and this is thought to have been at Carlisle, although it is fair to say that other places may also have a claim. The suggestion of a regional administrative function at Carlisle, however, does receive some support from a much earlier document. A letter discovered at Vindolanda, attributed to the early second century, refers to a man named 'Annius Equester, the centurion in charge of the region at Carlisle'. Taken at face value, this suggests that by the earliest years of the second century, Carlisle was already acting as some sort of regional centre.

Life in Roman Carlisle

Bed bugs, fleas and lice were endemic in ancient times, and this is as true of *Luguvalium* as of any other settlement. Not only have examples dating to these periods been unearthed in Carlisle, but careful examination of the soils has also revealed parasites, including the whipworm, which lived in the guts of humans, while other species that are specific to animals are also known. None of these pests would have been the cause of disease or illness if present in small numbers, but dysentery and other problems of the lower bowel could have occurred if the worm infestation was heavy. Life would certainly have been less comfortable by the standards of today.

The waterlogged soils of Carlisle that led to the preservation of plant and wood remains are also responsible for the survival of such delicate organisms as insects. Spiders, flies and many varieties of beetles have been discovered, and these provide an insight into the way in which our ancestors lived. Stables and cow byres, then as now, were breeding grounds for those types of beetle favouring rotting materials. These buildings were periodically cleaned out. In some cases the resulting filth was dumped outside in the yards, on other occasions it was doubtless carted out and spread on the fields. It would seem that the people of *Luguvalium* kept their buildings relatively clean inside. Despite the preference for earth floors, rubbish was not allowed to accumulate inside although small items did, on occasion, get trampled in.

Decorative shoulder piece from a Roman leather garment

Outside, the ground conditions were different. Evidence obtained from a study of the plant remains shows that many nooks and crannies beside and between buildings were colonized by weeds. Nettles, dock, daisies, buttercups and many other species flourished, forming traps for items lost by accident or deliberately thrown away. Areas subject to regular trampling were colonized by species such as plantains, while the numerous puddles attracted both plant and insect species with preferences for wet ground. Faeces, of both human and animal origin, have also been discovered, but there were no significant accumulations except in latrines. This may imply that the people of Roman Carlisle realized the value of faecal matter as a growing medium and, as with stable manure, collected it up for manuring the fields.

The basis of the economy was farming, and the local population, both in Carlisle and its environs, must have been geared to the production of surpluses for there was a substantial element in the population, the soldiers and the craftsmen, who were non-food producers.

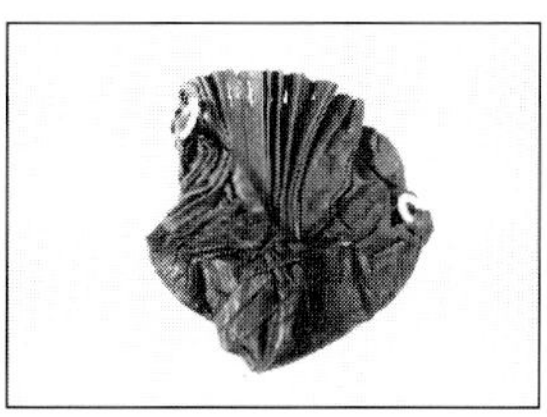

A Roman leather purse found in the fort at Annetwell Street

Two basic commodities were essential: cereal crops and the products of stock-raising. The staple cereals were various varieties of wheat, such as bread wheat and spelt, and barley. Emmer wheat, oats and rye have also been identified. As yet we do not know where the crops were grown, but from the presence of chaff it would appear likely that some barley at least was grown in the area, and a consideration of soil types suggests that the Eden Valley and an area between Knockupworth and Kirkbampton, including Grinsdale and Burgh by Sands, were the principal sources. The presence of other arable weeds may also indicate local production and, in the case of the poisonous corncockle that has to be removed by hand, there is some indication that grain processing took place in Carlisle itself. Insect remains, particularly of grain pests, point to local storage, while the querns, or millstones, and the carbonized grain found in various locations indicate the milling of flour on the spot before being baked into bread. Whereas much of the wheat was almost certainly intended for human consumption as bread, perhaps decorated with seeds of the opium poppy, the barley was probably used both for malting (or in a gruel) and as an animal feed. The remains of oats and rye are not sufficiently numerous to indicate local production and they may not have been more than weeds.

Meat, but not fish, was a key item in the local diet. Beef and mutton, with some lamb and smaller amounts of young pigs were provided by the local animal population. Indeed the soldiers in the fort

This fully grown Dexter bull is the nearest modern equivalent to the locally bred Celtic shorthorn of Roman times

at Annetwell Street seem to have had a particular penchant for lamb and sucking-pig. These species were supplemented occasionally by venison, mostly from red deer, wild whitefronted and barnacle geese and the odd hare. The older cattle, sheep and goats were probably used to supply milk and cheese.

Although fish bones are sometimes present, namely eel, salmon and trout, with the less common haddock, cod and plaice, their rarity is puzzling for an area so close to the Solway Firth and the rich resources of the River Eden. This is matched by the equally rare occurrence of coastal plants.

Animals were, of course, a ready supply of other raw materials: hides for clothing, tentage, belts, shield covers, containers; wool; bones for boiling up into gruels and soups as well as for a variety of pins, handles, and weaving tablets among other things. No useful raw material would have been discarded, and there were doubtless craftsmen specializing in leather goods or bone and horn objects.

Industrial production was small in scale. Indeed, large-scale industrial production was quite alien to Roman Britain. Evidence of crafts and industry is less well represented in the archaeological record. Hearths and ovens at Blackfriars Street and in The Lanes testify to some form of activity, but the nature of the craft is not known. Outside the main area of occupation, close to the River Caldew, a substantial dump of 'waste' pottery implies the presence of pottery kilns close by.

It is difficult to estimate the importance of trade with areas outside

A Roman basket, viewed from the underside, found blocking a drain in the gateway of the Roman fort at Annetwell Street

the region. Imported goods are clearly present. They include pots made in Yorkshire, Dorset, and the Peterborough area, for instance, as well as in various places in France and the Rhine Valley. The large amphorae, or storage vessels from southern Spain, probably arrived full of food or drink. Sardines, olives, fish-paste (*garum*) or wine, for example, may have arrived either this way or in large wooden barrels such as the one discovered in Keay's Lane. Other items, such as the mass-produced metalwares, brooches, rings, semi-precious stones (*intaglii*), and glassware, could mostly, if not all, be the products of craftsmen operating elsewhere in Britain.

Although many of these items are commonly found, they may not have been significant items of trade. A few itinerant pedlars could have accounted for much of the jewellery sold in the town, and the military may have had its own supplies sent up by land or sea.

There is plentiful evidence of religion in Roman Carlisle in the form of inscriptions and sculpture, but apart from one early building in The Lanes, no temples have been discovered so far. From within the Roman fort comes a crude representation of Hercules with his club, and a fragment of a fine panel bearing a representation of the owl,

Tombstone commemorating the death of Flavius Antigonus Papias, a citizen of Greece, and possibly a Christian. It was discovered in the nineteenth century near the London Road

associated with Minerva. A recent discovery at Carlisle Castle includes an altar dedicated to the principal Roman gods, Jupiter, Juno and Mars, while elsewhere in Carlisle there are hints of a temple to Mithras. Some of the smaller religious figures may have been household shrines. Celtic deities are also represented in the form of inscriptions recording local gods such as Belatucadros, while the Roman name for Carlisle, *Luguvalium*, preserves a Celtic element in the name *Luel*.

It is likely that there was a small, scattered indigenous population in the vicinity of Carlisle in the first century AD, but no evidence has so far come to light about where these people lived. The arrival of the Romans probably witnessed a considerable influx of people, the majority of whom would have been foreigners, soldiers serving with the army, provincial officials, or merchants. They include Annius Equester, the centurion in charge of the Carlisle region in the early second century, someone called Iulianus, and Flavius Antigonus Papias, a citizen of Greece, who died here aged about forty, probably in the fourth century. Others may have come from other parts of Britain. A third element would have been composed of people of local extraction attracted to the new fort and settlement of *Luguvalium* for economic and/or social reasons.

When Hadrian's Wall was built the number of foreigners living locally probably increased sharply, and this may have had the effect of increasing the local civilian population. As time went on, however, the size of the foreign element may have become diluted as soldiers serving both on Hadrian's Wall, and possibly in the Carlisle fort, were recruited from Britain. Indeed, many may have been locals. By the end of the Roman period it was likely that there were relatively few foreigners living here, except perhaps for senior officers and a few traders.

It is difficult to say how large the population of Roman Carlisle was at any point in time. Population estimates for Roman Britain vary considerably, and even when we know the size of forts, and can therefore estimate the size of the garrison, documents preserved at Vindolanda show that the 'paper' strength may be substantially more than the actual strength. Thus, even if the fort at Carlisle could theoretically hold a garrison of five hundred, it is probable that the actual numbers present for much of the time were rather less. Doubtless the size of the fighting force depended on the immediacy of hostile threats and on frontier policy at any one time. Thus, during a period of peace the numbers may have declined, while a period of hostility, or of troops advancing into or withdrawing from Scotland, may have resulted in the population swelling considerably.

However, during the second and third centuries it would probably be safe to assume a non-military population of Carlisle as numbering in the hundreds rather than thousands. The question of who they were is more difficult to answer. It can be assumed that the population included men, women and children, that a small element was relatively prosperous, another element comprised slaves and poor people, and that the others in the middle, perhaps the largest element, had sufficient resources to sustain themselves and their dependants.

Roman Carlisle was a focal point in the locality but it did not stand alone, isolated from the other settlements. *Luguvalium* would have been inextricably linked in with the rural settlements nearby. Indeed, it may well have been these rural sites that provided many of the basic food resources needed to sustain the soldiers and craftsmen of Carlisle.

Tombstone of a seated lady holding a fan and with an arm round a boy. It was found at Murrell Hill in 1878

Little is known about the rural hinterland in the immediate vicinity of Carlisle largely because much is now buried beneath modern suburbs stretching about 3 km from the city centre in most directions. Immediately beyond the built-up area, aerial photography, combined with a limited amount of fieldwork, shows that much of the landscape in ancient times was covered with field systems bounded by trees,

Aerial photograph of a 'native' farmstead on the Solway Plain. The dark lines are the filled-in enclosure ditches

dykes, hedges and trackways. At intervals within the fields were small farmsteads. Some of these farmsteads may be prehistoric or post-Roman in date, too few having been investigated to be certain as yet. Some are Roman, however, as excavation has demonstrated.

The typical Roman 'native' farmstead was set inside a ditched and embanked or fenced enclosure, which varied in plan. Within the enclosure there were the farmstead buildings, doubtless used for both domestic and agricultural needs. Some buildings were circular and are known as round-houses; these are part of the pre-Roman building tradition. Other buildings with a rectangular plan betray Roman influence. Outside the buildings, but within the enclosure, cobbled yards, drains, and other areas divided by fences were the 'working' areas of the farm. These enclosures were the homes of farmers and their families.

It is impossible at present to distinguish degrees of social status within the rural community. In many other parts of Britain Roman villas, which are basically farms or estate centres, are taken as representing the wealthy end of the social spectrum. Such villas are

A general view of excavations in progress on a 'native' site dating to the second century at the Cumberland Infirmary

often conspicuously Roman in that they have centrally heated rooms, a bath-house, painted plastered walls, and elaborate floors. There are only two villas in Britain north of Yorkshire and Lancashire, and both are east of the Pennines. No villas are known in Cumbria, but this should not lead us to suppose that none existed. It is possible that in one or two places, especially in the immediate environs of Carlisle where there was a modest degree of wealth, one or two of the better-off farmers may have resided in buildings with rather more Roman appointments than was the case in the humbler ditched enclosures.

Archaeology shows that many of the items typical of Roman life in towns, for example, pottery and glass vessels, coins, metal jewellery and metal attachments for boxes and clothing, are much less common at these rural sites. It is not clear why this should be. It is possible, for instance, that the people of the countryside were too poor to afford them. Alternatively, for cultural reasons, they may have deliberately chosen not to furnish their homes and decorate themselves in the same way as the people of the town and the soldiers did. They were, after all, part of Celtic society, in which we know from written sources that wealth was often measured in terms of numbers of cattle, or acres of land held, rather than by the number of Roman dishes displayed on the table.

CHAPTER TWO

Arthur, St Cuthbert and the Vikings

The End of a Roman Town

In the previous chapter we have seen how the Roman settlement, whether an 'urban' community or not in the mid-Roman period, nevertheless achieved a certain density of occupation and relative wealth and status. This achievement was not to last; during the fourth and subsequent centuries the nature of the settlement seems to have changed. These centuries represent one of the mysteries of Carlisle; they are missing links in the story.

The Roman fort was abandoned by the military in AD 330–40, but if the coins and pottery datable to the later fourth century are taken at face value, occupation in some form may have been sustained into the 370s, but probably not much later. The stone sheds which were erected over, and utilized part of, the former barrack walls are not the same as the so-called 'chalet' structures known at Housesteads and other Hadrian's Wall sites. At Stanwix, on the opposite side of the River Eden, the fate of the fort and its attendant settlement is still a mystery. Given the history of the other Hadrian's Wall forts, however, it would be surprising if Stanwix did not continue to be occupied in some form into the latter half of the fourth century.

The removal of the garrison from the fort in Carlisle in the first half of the fourth century could have acted as the catalyst for a gradual depopulation of the town. On the assumption that it was the presence of the military that provided much of the economic and social underpinning for the town's existence, the removal of the soldiers could have been disastrous. However, as we do not know to what extent the fort was fully garrisoned in the late third and early fourth centuries, so we cannot be sure when the process of decline began.

At Blackfriars Street, fourth-century Roman coins and pottery in association with buildings show occupation continuing for some time into the fifth century, well after the official Roman withdrawal from Britain. At 66–8 Scotch Street excavations revealed a gold coin, a *solidus* dating to the period AD 388–92, in the underfloor central heating ducts of a house. Here too we can be confident that this building remained in use long after the Roman withdrawal.

On at least two sites, therefore, we can be reasonably sure of fifth-century occupation. The evidence from elsewhere is less clear cut. It could be argued, on the basis of coins, pottery and other finds, that the picture of a sizeable thriving community after 370 or 380 cannot be sustained. This view can be supported by asserting that the economic consequences of the removal of the soldiers from the fort must have been considerable. No longer were military pay chests arriving in the town. There was no garrison to feed and official communications entailing couriers and the transport of supplies and equipment would have dried up. Any market function the Roman town could have performed may have dwindled. The withdrawal of the military effectively removed the need for a concentration of settlement.

On the other hand it would be dangerous to accept that view too readily. To argue for a decline in the town from the absence, or small quantities, of Roman coins, pottery and Roman knick-knacks presupposes that the people of Carlisle at the end of the Roman occupation had a use for them. It is possible that the local demand for such items collapsed not because nobody lived here, but because the loss of the military precipitated a change towards more traditional values. Within that scenario, coinage had no place as a medium of exchange, and pottery vessels for storing, preparing, or serving food must have been supplanted by other utensils.

The truth probably lies somewhere in the middle. The years between about AD 300 and 500 could well have witnessed settlement depopulation as the economic and social fabric declined. From the fourth century onwards we can suppose that wealth was measurable in cattle and land rather than in coins or other Roman 'gewgaws'. Dietary changes could have followed. Any access to exotic foods, facilitated by the Roman economic network and formerly enjoyed by the masses, may have dried up. The declining use of pottery containers may also betoken a shift in the methods of food preparation and cooking, and the types of food consumed.

The settlement of Carlisle was in the process of change. The process seems to have involved the gradual abandonment and collapse of many buildings, but some of the principal roads continued to function,

A gold coin (*solidus*) from the reign of Valentinian II (388–92) found during excavations at 66–8 Scotch Street in 1989

doubtless serving isolated pockets of activity. Some of the buildings in the town may have become parts of larger estates, perhaps run from other centres, while in other instances buildings in the town may themselves have become the foci of estates. That many estates continued to flourish is supported by the evidence of pollen diagrams taken from mosses in many parts of northern Britain. The evidence from around Carlisle, and indeed Cumbria as a whole, is not as full as it is for areas east of the Pennines, but the picture is nevertheless broadly consistent. It shows many parts of the country that were cleared of woodlands in the fourth century continued to be kept clear of wood regeneration throughout the fifth and sixth centuries. In the Lake District, and at Bolton Fell, just a few miles north-east of Carlisle, farming seems to have been particularly vigorous.

It is possible that this is the context in which we should view the early life of St Patrick. In letters written much later in life, Patrick tells us that he came from a place known as *Bannavem Taburniae*, which scholars today equate with the Hadrian's Wall fort of Birdoswald (*Banna*). His father and grandfather, he tells us, were deacon and

The Roman fort at Birdoswald showing posts marking the position of a hall believed to be Dark Age in date

priest respectively of the local church and owned a small estate. The implication is that Patrick's family were people with a modest degree of status and possibly wealth in the local community. It would not stretch credulity too far to envisage them as being connected in some way with a place like Carlisle in the decades on either side of AD 400, especially as his father had official status as a *decurion*.

If we are correct in identifying *Bannavem Taburniae* with Birdoswald, we have good evidence for the presence of Christianity in this locality. Despite the brave attempts by some scholars to see Carlisle as the home of St Ninian, however, and to see it as the centre of a late Roman diocese, there is no archaeological or written evidence to support the claim so far.

The Age of Arthur

What happened next is literally a mystery. The time between the end of Roman rule and the arrival of the Anglo-Saxons in the seventh century is one of the most tantalizing in British archaeology. It is confused with myth and counter-myth about semi-historical figures such as King Arthur, and hagiographic traditions concerned with dynastic rivalries and the emergence of British kingdoms in the generations before the expansion of Northumbria in the seventh century.

There is a local tradition, for example, that King Arthur was in some way connected with the area, and it has been suggested recently that he was born at Caerlaverock, near Annan, and gave his name to Arthuret where, it is alleged, he was buried. It has also been alleged that Carlisle was King Arthur's Camelot and that his last great battle, at Camlann, was fought somewhere nearby, perhaps at the Hadrian's Wall fort of *Camboglanna* (Castlesteads).

The King Arthur stories are a deeply embedded and very rich seam in English literature mined by people in all walks of life. The literary merits of the Arthurian tales are considerable but their accuracy as historical records has been frequently questioned. As a result there is a dispute among historians as to whether Arthur ever existed. Ultimately the arguments for the reality or not of King Arthur rest on a detailed analysis of the written sources, taking account of such questions as their dating and the reasons why they were written, as well as understanding the language and terminology employed.

This is not the place to set out arguments for or against King Arthur. Suffice it to say that the present writer believes that a man named Arthur, who was a great warleader, probably existed, perhaps in an official capacity or as a mercenary, in the late fifth or early sixth centuries. Out of the great mass of literary sources there are just two near-contemporary documents that may be used in support. In the Welsh Easter Annals is the record that in the 'Year 93. Strife of Camlann in which Arthur and Modred died'. This laconic annal probably belongs to the year AD 510. It provides us with no other information about Arthur, Modred or Camlann but it was clearly felt to be of such importance as to have impressed itself on the mind of the annalist. The Annals also record that Arthur's last great victory took place at Badon, but this battle does not feature in the battle-list contained in the so-called Arthurian section of another early source, the *Historia Brittonum* of Nennius.

The second source is the epic poem known as *The Gododdin* commemorating the exploits of a warband from Lothian and their last disastrous battle, thought to have been near Catterick, North Yorkshire. One of the deceased members of this warband had many brave qualities but, it is said, 'he was not Arthur'. The Annals and *The Gododdin* are the only two written sources that refer to Arthur and which were compiled within a century of his death.

Some writers have attempted to locate Arthur in north Britain on the basis of places mentioned in the battle-list supplied by Nennius and the reference to Camlann in the Annals. These attempts amount to little more than guesswork. The seventh battle on Nennius's list took place at the wood of Celyddon. This means the Caledonian woods, which in this context refers to Scotland, perhaps the lowlands, rather than the area north of the Great Glen. The other places on the list are equally vague or more so, and in many cases more than one interpretation is possible. The reference to Camlann in the Welsh Annals is a little more specific, and is generally believed to be the Roman Hadrian's Wall fort of *Camboglanna*, now equated with Castlesteads, near Brampton. There is no historical evidence to connect Arthur with either Caerlaverock, Arthuret or Carlisle, and the idea that Camelot was at Carlisle is pure fiction. The arguments advanced by many of the adherents to the tales are based entirely on unfounded assumptions and a misunderstanding of the nature of the source material.

In north Britain, traditions recorded in early Welsh poetry dating to the late sixth and early seventh centuries refer to many tribal groupings presided over by kings, but this period is as difficult and confusing to understand as the preceding so-called Arthurian period.

It is clear, from the early Welsh poems of Taliesin and the genealogies, that the Carlisle area was contested during internecine

Aerial photograph of Arthuret church. The present church dates to the seventeenth century but an earlier one is known to have occupied the site. This may be the site of the great battle of AD 573

wars in the sixth century. In AD 573 a great battle took place at Arthuret, some 7 miles north of Carlisle, between different branches of the Edinburgh-based Coeling dynasty. This battle was referred to many times in various poems and was clearly regarded as being ferocious and highly significant, and although its importance now is difficult to assess, it can be surmised that control of the region around the Esk and Eden, vitally important in strategic terms, could have been one of the points at issue. Another aspect may have been control of Wardlaw fort just above Caerlaverock, the 'city of the lark's nest' also mentioned in the early poems.

The battle of Arthuret took place within the British kingdom of Rheged that was located, according to the weight of scholarly opinion, around the Solway Firth. The former Roman settlement of Carlisle was well within its orbit. The best known king of Rheged was Urien. Even though the name Urien, or Urbgen as he is referred to in the genealogies, means 'city born', and *could* allude to Carlisle, we do not know what the poets meant by the term.

Urien's fame extended over a wide area and to some extent this may have derived from his distinguished ancestry, being a member of the Coeling dynasty. Although Urien is not specifically associated with Carlisle, in the poems of Taliesin he is mentioned in connection with *Llwyfenydd* (Lyvennet) in the Eden Valley. He was regarded as a great king, the lord of Christendom, a raider of cattle and as a successful warlord. He took part in and won many battles, especially in the nascent Bernicia (Northumberland), and probably united some of the warring parties. He was eulogized as Urien of Catraeth (Catterick, North Yorkshire). His sons, Owain and Rhun, were also distinguished, but ultimately the British resistance to the Anglo-Saxons' advance in Northumbria crumbled away.

Analysis of many of the Welsh poems and traditions of this remote period show that they originated not in Wales but in Cumbria, the very name of which is synonymous with Wales. Some of these poems and genealogies were transmitted orally, but some were written down as linguistic studies have shown. Certain scholars believe this took place in Carlisle although firm evidence for the status of Carlisle in the sixth century is generally lacking. Nevertheless, the weight of evidence suggests that there was, within the Solway area, a relatively high status settlement, perhaps a monastic *scriptorium*, in which these tales were written down.

Celtic churchmen were active in the Solway region in the sixth century, one of the best known being St Kentigern, one of the sons of Urien. Recent excavations at Hoddom, Dumfriesshire, have yielded dated monastic buildings that may be contemporary with Kentigern who was there in AD 573, but so far there is no direct evidence to link Christianity with Carlisle, although Urien and Rhun, one of his other sons, were Christian, Rhun being a priest. Other Celtic churchmen were also active, and later in the seventh century we know of the existence of hermits, such as St Hereberht (Herbert), who met St Cuthbert on the latter's second visit to Carlisle, probably in AD 686. St Hereberht lived the life of an ascetic on an island in Derwentwater.

If Carlisle was a high status settlement, a not improbable suggestion, we may expect to discover some artefacts such as imported glass, pottery or metalwork that reflect it. So far, however, the archaeological evidence from Carlisle and the locality for the fifth and sixth centuries is scanty. At Blackfriars Street was found part of a military belt fitting attributed to the late fourth or fifth centuries. At the cathedral, dumps of earth laid down in the ninth century included a brooch attributable to the fifth to seventh centuries. This so-called 'dark earth' overlay other features, including the remains of a building constructed with massive posts, which may be of similar or slightly later date. The dearth of finds for this period may be more apparent than real, however. The excavations may not have been located in those parts of Carlisle occupied at that time, and it is also possible that the main focus of settlement, the local centre of power, was situated elsewhere. The records of the battle of Arthuret, for example, suggest that one power-base was somewhere between Arthuret church,

Netherby and Liddel Motte. The fort 'at the lark's nest', Wardlaw fort above Caerlaverock, may be another, but in the absence of firm archaeological evidence it is difficult to be certain what kind of settlement was used by these warring parties. To what extent would an old Roman settlement, even one such as the fort at Carlisle (or Stanwix) with defences that were still usable, have been attractive? Recent excavations at the Hadrian's Wall fort at Birdoswald suggest that some post-Roman activity is present, but for many of the petty kings recorded in the poems and genealogies, defended hilltops may have been the preferred option, as was the case both in the pre-Roman Iron Age in parts of England and Wales, and in Pictish Scotland in the sixth to eighth centuries.

St Cuthbert at Carlisle

In the end the warring and feuding between members of the Coeling dynasty came to nothing. Between Aethelfrith of Northumbria's great victory in Liddesdale in AD 603, and 638 when the future King Oswy married Urien's great-granddaughter Rhiemmelth, the kingdom of Rheged was peacefully absorbed into the expanding Northumbrian kingdom. For over two hundred years thereafter much of England, west of the Pennines, and southern Scotland formed part of a single political unit. Perhaps the most enduring aspect of this English expansion was the arrival of Roman Catholic missionaries spreading the word of God, a mission magnificently attested in the late seventh or early eighth century crosses at Bewcastle and Ruthwell, and numerous other examples of Anglian workmanship.

In AD 685, two years before his death, St Cuthbert, Bishop of Lindisfarne, visited Carlisle where the queen of Northumbria was awaiting news of the fate of her husband, King Ecgfrith. In succeeding centuries the cult of St Cuthbert was to give rise to more church and holy well dedications bearing his name in Cumbria than any other saint. While he was here St Cuthbert founded a monastery.

Although we know very little about this monastery it is thought to lie within the vicinity of St Cuthbert's church and the cathedral. It is possible that the building underneath the 'dark earth' at the cathedral mentioned above, is part of the monastery. The view that the monastery was very close by is reinforced by the discovery in the nineteenth century of fragments of eighth-century sculptured crosses from the cathedral precincts and St Cuthbert's Lane. Such crosses are almost always identified with monasteries at this date. Together with the proximity of St Cuthbert's church, whose dedication and unusual alignment imply a very early foundation, the crosses serve to identify the area as the general position of the Anglian monastery.

During his visit St Cuthbert and the queen were shown the city walls and a wondrous fountain by Waga, the *praepositus*, and the citizens. These are very important and almost contemporary references. They not only tell us of the existence of a nunnery presided over by the queen's sister, but they also provide hints about the fabric of the settlement and one of its leading members. Some scholars have been misled into thinking that the Roman city survived into the seventh century. Such references are difficult to interpret and, in view of the known archaeology, should not be taken at face value. So far neither Roman city walls nor a fountain, and its necessary aqueduct, have been discovered. The authors of this information, Bede and the Anonymous Author of the Life of St Cuthbert, may have been referring to other features. The city walls, for example, could have been those known to have defended the fort, while fountains, together with holy wells, both aspects of the ancient pagan veneration of water, occur widely as place-names and in the literature associated with saints. Exactly what St Cuthbert saw is not certain, but it could have been a spring or a well, of which there were many fine stone examples in the Roman town.

The Bewcastle Cross, erected within the Roman outpost fort in the late seventh or early eight century, is one of the finest examples of Northumbrian art in northern Britain

Carlisle was also part of an extensive estate belonging to the monastery, some 15 miles in circumference. The estate was probably granted by King Ecgfrith to St Cuthbert on the latter's inauguration as bishop. The reference to Waga, whose title *praepositus* may be roughly translated as a reeve, is of interest in this respect. Reeves were important figures in Anglo-Saxon England and were often the equivalent of today's estate manager.

The importance of the settlement of Carlisle at this time in cultural, social and economic terms is difficult to assess because the historical sources provide little direct evidence and because remains of the period are scanty. We should remember, however, that Carlisle was part of a network of Northumbrian monastic institutions that developed a very distinct cultural identity during the seventh and eighth centuries. It may not have enjoyed the international reputation that places like Jarrow and Monkwearmouth had, but there is no reason to believe that it lacked paintings, wall hangings and other adornments, although perhaps not on the scale of Wilfred's churches at Hexham and Ripon.

The settlement probably consisted of much more than a collection of monastic buildings. The distribution of archaeological finds implies occupation along two of the main roads of the former Roman town.

The fabric of the settlement is still unknown, however, and awaits future archaeological discoveries, but it is clear, from the descriptions of St Cuthbert's visit, that remains of the Roman city were still in evidence.

Archaeological evidence for the period at Carlisle is scanty. In 1977 traces of a timber building were revealed at Blackfriars Street, close to St Cuthbert's church, but its function remains unknown. Excavations at the cathedral have revealed a small number of objects dating to this period including pins, a silver garter hook, a silver coin known as a *sceat* dating to the eighth century, and metal strap-ends, one of which may be Carolingian and have originated in France. Other archaeological discoveries include a number of timber-lined pits, not deep enough to be wells but which were nevertheless purpose-built structures, dated to the late eighth or very early ninth century. A few fragments of metalwork, glass and a clay loom weight have also been found, as well as two fragments of clay moulds for making bronze strap-ends.

The most frequently occurring objects are small copper alloy coins known as *stycas*, of which over fifty have been discovered mostly on the western side of the city centre, north and south of the cathedral, as well as along the main east–west Roman road. These small crude coins are a Northumbrian coinage, some of which were almost

A large pit, lined with oak timbers cut from trees felled between AD 770 and 803, found at Castle Street, Carlisle, in 1982

certainly minted in York but, given the distribution of the various types, they may also have been minted in a few other important centres. Carlisle is one such centre, and its claim to be a mint is reinforced by the discovery of a one-sided *styca* that could be a trial-piece from the local mint. These *stycas*, dating largely from around AD 800–850, were minted in the names of the Northumbrian kings, but there were also a number of ecclesiastical issues, of which the Carlisle trial-piece may be an example. Confirmation that Carlisle had its own mint in the ninth century would further underline its significance and add an interesting dimension to our understanding of the political situation.

The Viking Age

The monastic community and its settlement probably continued to function through to the late ninth century, when it is said to have been sacked by the Vikings. This event probably took place in the year AD 876, shortly after the Danes moved north from their winter base at Repton into Northumbria and began a systematic takeover of the Northumbrian kingdom under their great leader, Halfdan. The sacking of Carlisle marks the end of the monastery founded nearly two centuries before by St Cuthbert, but it does not mark the end of Carlisle's Cuthbert community. The Abbot of Carlisle, Eadred, linked up with his north-eastern colleagues who, at about this time, began a seven-year exile, wandering around the north with the incorrupt body of St Cuthbert seeking refuge from the Danes. Eadred seems to have become a leading light among his colleagues, for his name occurs several times. It was he who finally secured a resting place for the body at Chester-le-Street in AD 883. One suspects that Eadred was a canny fellow with a politician's instincts for survival, for a few years later, according to John of Worcester, in AD 895, Eadred appears again, but this time he was inaugurating the Danish King Guthfrith.

John of Worcester also went on to say that Carlisle then lay waste, and was deserted for some two hundred years after the attack, although this now seems unlikely. Possibly in the 940s Catroe, a Scottish saint, was making his way to York from Scotland and was taken to the *civitas Loidem*, which is almost certainly a simple error for Carlisle (*Loidem* was Leeds) that was said to be 'on the boundary of the Northmen and the Cumbrians'. We hear nothing else about Carlisle, but its description as a *civitas* allows us to infer that it was a place of some significance. One interpretation of the confused political map of the tenth century is that Carlisle lay between the territories of the king of Scots, Constantine II mac Aed, and Owen, king of the Cumbrians. By the late eleventh century Carlisle was within the kingdom of the Scots.

What is clear is that Cumbria, however it was defined, became of great strategic importance, and control of the area was crucial both to the territorial ambitions of successive Scots kings and to the kings of England. Possession of Carlisle, which controls the main north–south land-route at the head of the Solway Firth, was vital, as was recognized by the Romans in former times and later by the English crown. Cumbria, and Carlisle in particular, was, as one writer has put it, 'a stepping stone' between the Norwegians in the west and the Danes to the east.

Evidence of Viking settlement in Cumbria occurs in the form of place-names, fine sculptured crosses such as that at Gosforth on the coast, gravecovers and other artefacts. The place-names are of mixed origin, reflecting the presence of immigrants from Scandinavia, the Gaelic north-west and the Danes in Yorkshire. Many of the place-names in the Eden Valley, and in the immediate vicinity of Carlisle, contain the very common Danish element *-by* (as in Upperby), indicating at the very least Danish influence if not Danes themselves. Relatively few Viking objects are known from Carlisle or the immediate vicinity, although the iron axe from Longsowerby, a rune-inscribed gold ring found in 1817 at Kingmoor, and the 1855 discovery at Scotby of silver ingots and coins thought to have been deposited in the 930s, are all worthy of mention. The numbers of crosses and hog-back gravestones is relatively sparse in Carlisle and its surrounding region, however, and this has led one scholar to suggest that the centre of power in the Anglo-Scandinavian period lay further south.

This conclusion, like that of John of Worcester, can also be questioned. Archaeological excavations immediately adjacent to the west end of the cathedral uncovered part of a cemetery dating to the tenth century. Three phases of cemetery usage can be discerned. Some burials were placed in slab-lined graves, and included both coffined burials and others without coffins. Nor were the people buried here mere peasants. Some may have been of higher status to judge by the metal belt fittings, the silver-capped whetstone, the gold toggle and iron coffin fittings. What their ethnic origins were is another matter. A consideration of some of the finds and methods of interment suggests connections with the Norse world of the Isle of Man, Ireland and Scandinavia, as well as Yorkshire and the Danelaw, and on this tenuous basis it could be suggested that the population of

Excavations outside Carlisle Cathedral in 1988 uncovered a Viking-age cemetery, seen here being excavated

tenth-century Carlisle included some immigrants, perhaps arriving here in the first wave of Norse migration to north-west England in the first or second decades of the tenth century. The old affiliations with the kingdom of Northumbria were lost and Carlisle, together with much of what today is known as Cumbria, became absorbed into different political groupings.

The burials excavated at the cathedral would have been adjacent to an important church, for which we have one other piece of evidence. This is a stone cross-head found in 1855 during repairs to one of the transepts. The church probably lies somewhere underneath the cathedral cloister or Fratry. It would have been a private church perhaps handed over, together with its lands and revenues, to a deserving member of the Danish host. There are slight hints of other churches as well. At Castle Street parts of two burials were discovered, one of which was dated by radiocarbon techniques to the period between the seventh and early eleventh centuries, and these probably indicate a church nearby. The site of the medieval chapel of St Alban, and St Cuthbert's church itself, are other candidates for churches of this period.

If we are right in supposing that there was more than one church in the Viking-age town, we have further evidence for the break-up of the former Northumbrian estate centre, a process which surely began with the political realignments affecting northern England after the onset of the Danish invasions in the 870s. This process was eventually to be completed in the twelfth century when the estates held by Dolfin and his brother Waldeve, sons of Gospatric, were probably transferred to the Normans Bochard and Ricard.

Elsewhere in Carlisle archaeologists can show that the Viking-age settlement was not just confined to the cathedral. In the Annetwell Street/Tullie House area, finds include a penny of Edgar, probably circulating in the period around AD 973–1000, a bone comb and a bone skate, while a fine enamelled disc brooch was discovered at Old Grapes Lane, and a bead at Scotch Street.

These Viking-period finds from Carlisle, although not as numerous as those of the preceding Anglian period, have a similar distribution, and indicate a settlement along the roads to the south and the east. Within this settlement the church or churches would have occupied an important role.

Another important element in the settlement would have been the residence of the lord. In 1092, when the Normans conquered Cumbria, the *Anglo-Saxon Chronicle* tells us that Dolfin, son of Earl Gospatric, was driven out of Carlisle. According to written

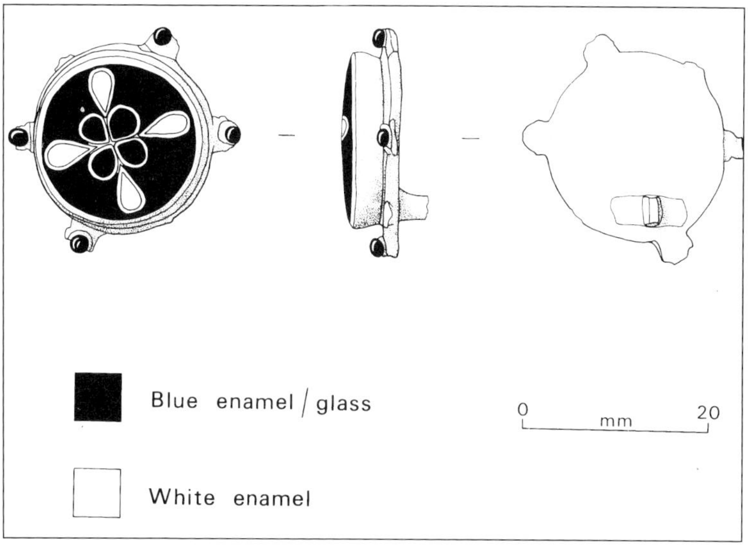

A disc brooch made of gilt bronze with enamel decoration dating to the tenth or eleventh centuries, found during excavations at Old Grapes Lane in 1981

sources both Gospatric, and by implication Dolfin, seem to have enjoyed powers that were almost regal, and their presence in Carlisle marks out the settlement as one of great importance. It possessed many of the attributes necessary to urban development including the presence of men of rank, the probability that there were several estates whose owners had property here even if they did not themselves live here, the dependence of the estates upon Carlisle in terms of the payment of tithes and other dues, its position on the road system, at least one major church and the possibility of others, and defensive potential. It is likely that Carlisle also performed a market function, and we may conclude that it was in many respects a proto-urban centre, if not an actual town. If we accept this, Carlisle is of even greater interest with regard to its position within the Scottish kingdom. There are no examples of towns known in Scotland before the twelfth century, although some scholars believe that proto-towns may have existed in the eleventh century at such places as Glasgow and St Andrews.

Definition of urban status at this time in Britain is largely based on how the Anglo-Saxons thought of towns. Law Codes enacted by various Anglo-Saxon kings, especially Aethelstan in the mid-tenth century, refer to such features as defences, the possession of a mint and the presence of burgesses as being crucial for a settlement to be regarded as a borough. None of these apply in Carlisle, which in any case lay outside the effective jurisdiction of the Anglo-Saxon kings.

On the basis of these criteria, therefore, Carlisle cannot be thought of as a town in the tenth or eleventh centuries. Nevertheless, circumstantial evidence suggests that Carlisle, whatever its status during the Dark Ages, was effectively a town by the time the Normans arrived.

CHAPTER THREE

The Normans to the Tudors

The Norman Settlement

In the year 1092, perhaps in May or June, King William II (Rufus), son of William the Conqueror, led his army northwards and drove out Dolfin from Carlisle. William's first task, on arriving in Carlisle, would have been the erection of a castle from which control could be exercised. William's castle is now difficult to identify with any certainty. It may have comprised a motte and bailey, that is a strong timber tower on top of a great mound of earth set within a defended enclosure. As there is no evidence for this, however, William may not have bothered with a motte, being content with buildings within an enclosure defended by a large bank and ditch.

Cumberland was parcelled out to eminent Norman and Breton lords. Carlisle lay within the lordship of Ranulf le Meschin, but other lordships were created nearby at Burgh by Sands, Gilsland and Liddel. These baronies with their castles formed a formidable defence for the English crown. The granting of land to lesser Norman lords is reflected in the names Botcherby, Harraby, Wiggonby, Tarraby, Etterby and others, in which the first element is Norman French in origin. The second element *-by* is Danish and may be a reflection of earlier settlement.

From the reign of Henry I the modern town of Carlisle gradually began to take shape. It was Henry who, on a visit to Carlisle in 1122, provided funds for the building of a castle and towers, probably a reference to the stone keep and city walls, and it was he who, in the same year, granted land for the foundation of the priory by Augustinian canons. Ten years later the diocese of Carlisle was carved out of the Bishop of Strathclyde's patrimony.

All this amounted to the consolidation of the Norman hold on Cumbria, which provided an increasingly difficult target for the Scottish kings. From the time William Rufus arrived in 1092 no Scottish king

Aerial photograph of Carlisle Castle

was able to mount a successful attack on the town, despite William the Lion's attempts in 1173–4 and the Bruces in the fourteenth century. But Carlisle was much more than a fortress although the king may have seen it largely in those terms. To the people of Carlisle it was the opportunities provided by Henry I, David I and Henry II, whose combined reigns spanned most of the twelfth century, which turned the settlement into a truly urban community. Carlisle became the economic, fiscal, judicial, social and religious focus for the county of Cumberland in a way not previously experienced.

A ground-floor room at Carlisle Castle showing some of the earliest Norman stonework including a blocked window

Part of this new-found prosperity was due to the mines at Alston, which were exploited for their silver. The silver was taken to Carlisle, where it was turned into coin when a mint was established here by 1135; Carlisle then became one of only three mints in the north, the others being at York and Durham. This alone testifies to the king's view of Carlisle's importance. The presence of the mint, closed in 1208 but re-established with four moneyers in 1247, together with the security afforded by the castle and the ring of defences in the outlying baronies, the presence of the sheriff, and the tremendous amount of activity that must have accompanied the simultaneous building of castle and priory, must have done wonders to boost the attractions of Carlisle as a market. Take the building programme, for example. This must have involved large numbers of labourers and craftsmen quarrying sandstone in the Eden Valley, stripping Roman remains for the usable stone, cutting down trees in Inglewood, carting the timber into the town, plastering walls, digging foundations. This was not a short term programme as medieval building campaigns such as this could be prolonged over several generations.

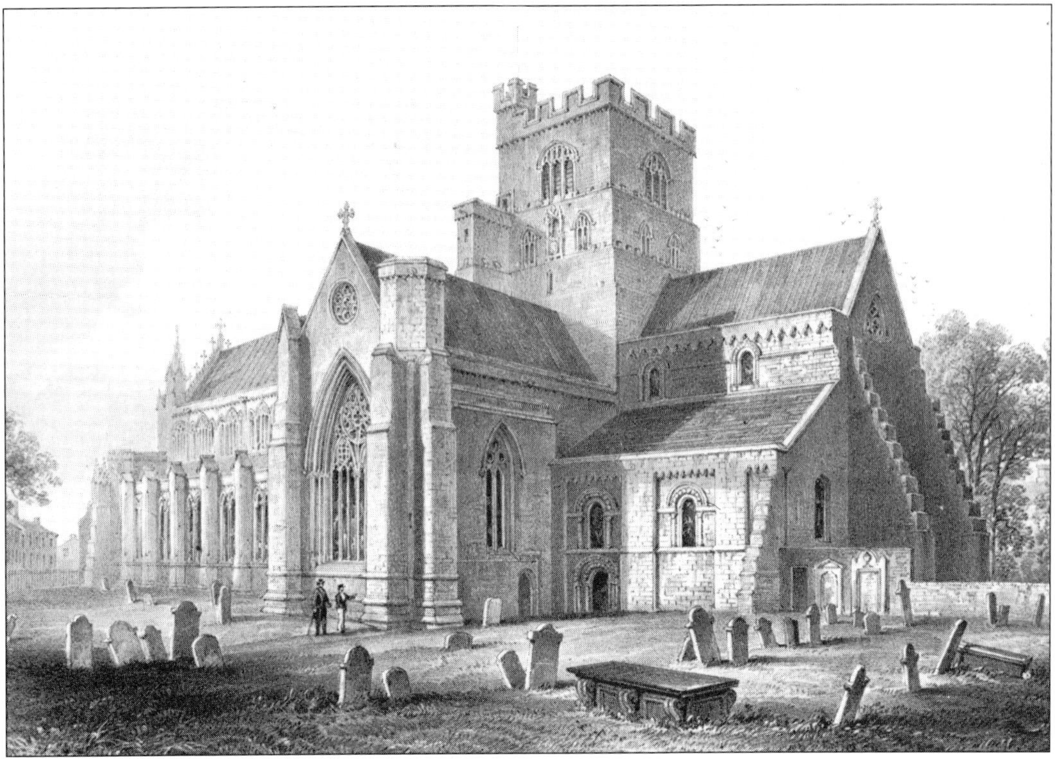

An engraving of Carlisle Cathedral. The earliest Norman work in the shortened nave, heavily restored in the nineteenth century, can be clearly seen

The foundation of the priory of Augustinian canons in 1122 initiated a particularly large-scale building programme at what is now the cathedral. Although doubtless housed in timber buildings initially, as excavations at another Augustinian house, at Norton in Cheshire, have shown, the priority of the canons was the building in stone of their church, followed by the Chapter House. The church must have been over 240 ft (80 m) in length, and would have looked quite different to the church of today. The seven-bay nave extended almost as far as the house now known as number 2 in the cathedral precinct, while the original east end, formed from three apses rather than being squared off, lies underneath the choir. Substantial, albeit restored, remains of the first Norman church erected in the middle decades of the twelfth century can be seen at the crossing and in the two surviving bays of the cathedral nave. Elsewhere, however, there is no Norman work visible. Indeed it is possible that the impetus for the building campaign slowed down in the long period after the death of the first bishop and prior, Adelulf, in 1156, during which the See was vacant.

The churches of St Cuthbert and St Alban, as well as the suburban church of Holy Trinity in Caldewgate, almost certainly witnessed building activity in the twelfth or thirteenth centuries, although not on as large a scale as at the priory. Little is known about the medieval church of St Cuthbert, which was entirely rebuilt in 1778, but excavations have located the lost church of St Alban on Scotch Street.

Other large-scale building works were put in hand in the thirteenth century. Not only did this affect the castle and the cathedral, where the choir was lengthened, but it also entailed the building of two friaries. Both groups of friars arrived in Carlisle in 1233. The Franciscans, or Greyfriars, began building in the area between Bank Street and Devonshire Street, while the Dominicans, or Blackfriars, first settled beyond the city walls in Botchergate, and moved to a more permanent site in Blackfriars Street in 1238. Both the Greyfriars and Blackfriars plots were almost certainly vacant and unencumbered by buildings. Very little is known about either of the friaries in Carlisle and nothing now survives to mark the spot, but excavations in 1977–8 in Blackfriars Street uncovered part of the Dominicans' church, together with fragmentary remains of other buildings thought to belong to those grouped around the cloister. Although both orders of friars had an arrangement of buildings around a cloister, thus presenting the appearance of a monastery, in fact the friars were much more worldly in their beliefs and practice. Both the Dominican and Franciscan churches, for example, would have looked quite different to normal churches. They were essentially preaching and teaching orders, for which they needed a church in which the maximum number of people could be accommodated with a clear view to the pulpit.

The excavations at Blackfriars Street also revealed part of the cemetery in which the remains of over two hundred people were uncovered. They included men, women, children and infants. Examination of the skeletal remains showed that men averaged 5 ft 7 in in height and women 5 ft 3 in. They suffered from tooth decay, as might be expected. Caries, abcesses and periodontal diseases are all recorded, as were traces of other diseases caused by bone infection. Some of these infections may have been caused by trauma or scurvy. Arthritis was present in several cases and there was one example of spina bifida. Other problems occurred as a result of violence, sometimes possibly through accident, while in other cases it may have been deliberate. There were several cases in which poor nutrition in childhood can be tentatively recognized. Many children survived childhood, however, but the numbers of people reaching the age of fifty and living beyond that were relatively small. If women survived

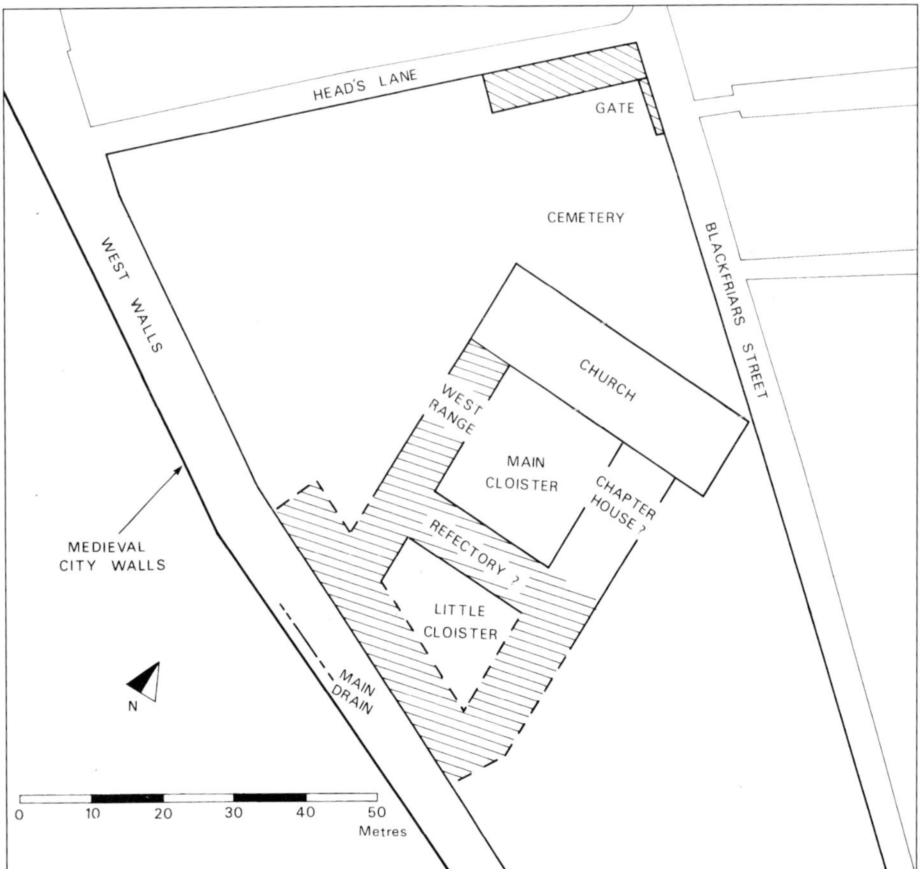
HEAD'S LANE
GATE
CEMETERY
BLACKFRIARS STREET
WEST WALLS
CHURCH
WEST RANGE
MAIN CLOISTER
CHAPTER HOUSE ?
REFECTORY ?
LITTLE CLOISTER
MEDIEVAL CITY WALLS
MAIN DRAIN
N
0
10
20
30
40
50
Metres

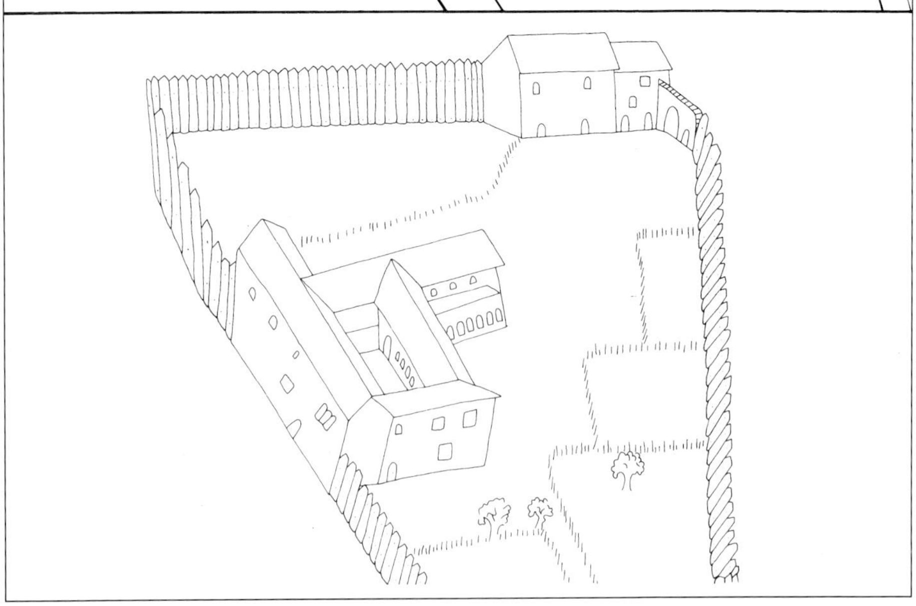

childbirth, a common cause of death in the medieval world, they seem to have lived to a similar age as men.

By the end of the thirteenth century the people of the city comprised not only Cumbrians, but also Norman French and Flemings, as well as others whose names betray a Celtic, Anglo-Saxon or Scandinavian origin. Many of these people must have been occupied in either building-related work or non-economic activities such as soldiers and clerics. The economy depended on merchants engaged in trade, a major aspect in the life of most medieval towns. Confirmation of the status of Carlisle and its role in the regional trade network is provided by the town charter given by Henry II in 1158.

Trade was regulated through the guild merchant, composed of the burgesses who were the richer members of the community. Trade took place through markets and fairs, many being local in scope, but markets to Ireland were exploited through the growth of small ports on the Cumberland coast. Indeed, by 1230 there was an Irish Street (*vicus Hibernicorum*) in Carlisle, and the Anglo-Scottish enclave in Dublin included men from Carlisle. One of the most important markets was in Scotland. Abbeys at Jedburgh, Holyrood and Melrose came to own properties in the town, and William the Lion told the monks of Holm Cultram that they could trade in wool and virtually anything they liked in any of his towns. Indeed, contact between Scotland and Cumberland was fostered by the church and by the Scottish king, who acquired property in many places after the border was eventually defined in 1237 at the Treaty of York. This is not to say that Carlisle did not trade with the rest of England, for there were substantial commercial contacts between Carlisle and Newcastle probably from the early twelfth century. Contacts also existed between Carlisle and York and north Yorkshire, as well as other places in Cumberland and Westmorland.

Fairs were held annually from 15 August for some fifteen days thereafter. The weekly market was in the centre of the city, around the present Greenmarket and Town Hall Square. The market was next to the cemetery of St Alban's Church, whose churchyard would have been used as much for secular activities as for the quiet contemplation and respect afforded nowadays. Goods passing through the Carlisle market would have included wool, salt, grain, dairy products, fish, leather, horses and doubtless many other smaller items. Sea-coal probably came from Whitehaven, squirrel skins from local woods, and iron from Egremont.

As in many places in England, one of the principal commodities was wool and cloth. Local wool was much sought after and was

The Dominican friary, Blackfriars Street, showing (top) a reconstructed plan and (bottom) an extract taken from the earliest map of Carlisle (1560)

Burials in the cemetery accompanying St Alban's church, Scotch Street, excavated in 1989

exported to the continent, and by the end of the thirteenth century Carlisle was a major focus for the textile trade as a market for raw and finished products, as a place to obtain woad and potash, and as a treatment centre with dyeworks and fulling mills. Indeed, the making of cloth was sufficiently lucrative as to attract other traders working on a part-time basis such as skinners, an apothecary and a goldsmith who were arraigned before the courts in 1292.

Given the climate and quality of soils in Cumbria, it is not surprising to learn that leather, too, was a major commodity. Stock-raising did not just supply meat to the butchers, but also hides and skins to the leather trade. Nor was it confined to cattle and sheep hides but lambs, goats, kids, squirrels, cats, hares, rabbits and foxes were also treated and used by curriers, sheath-makers, cobblers, shield-makers, saddlers, and glovers.

The buildings of the townsfolk are more difficult to envisage, largely because the written sources, so full for some aspects of life, rarely provide us with the detail. Few buildings in the town were made of stone. They included the priory and castle, and the

Map of Cumbria showing the directions of trade and goods exchanged in the thirteenth century

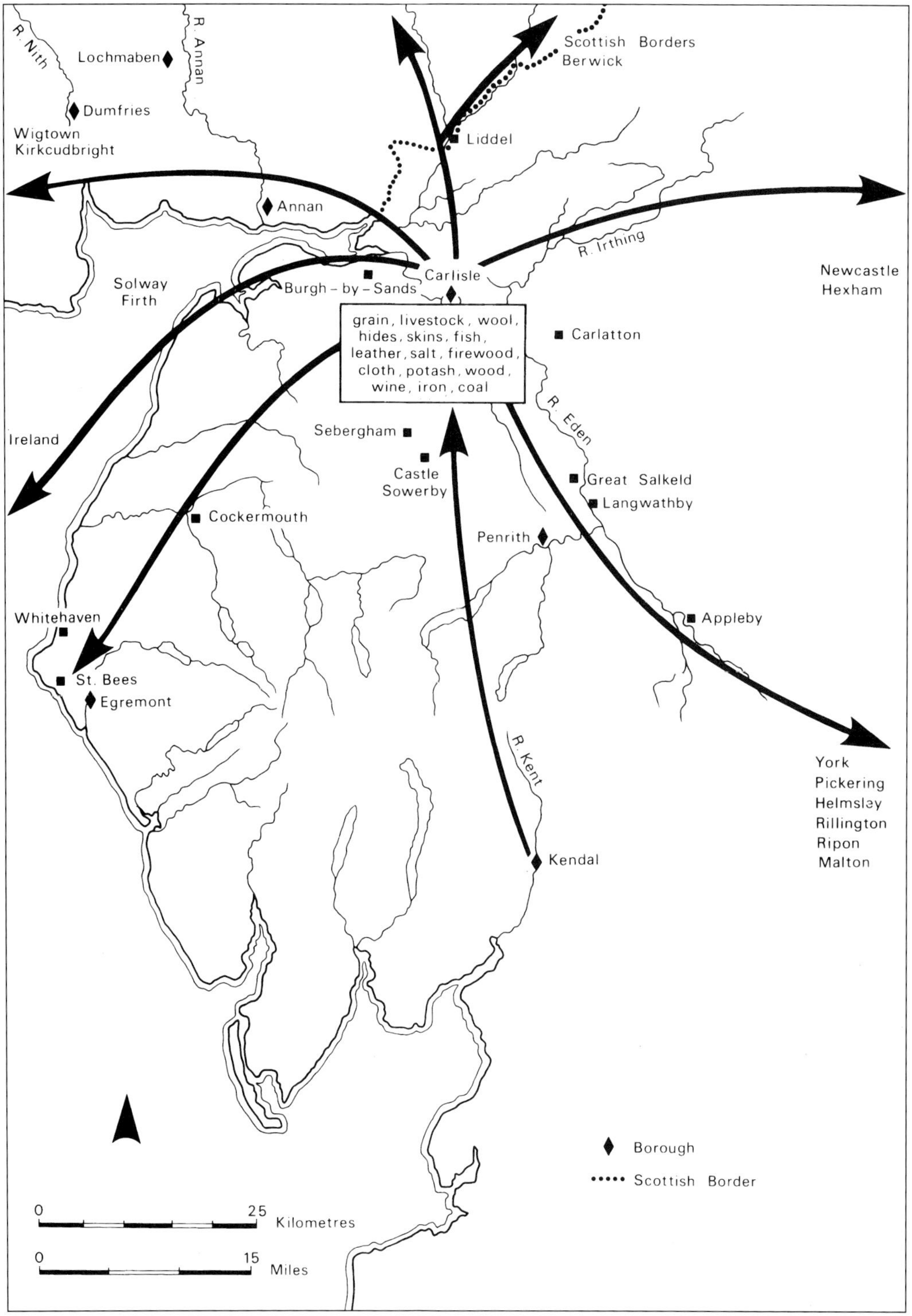
R. Nith
Lochmaben
R. Annan
Dumfries
Wigtown
Kirkcudbright
Scottish Borders
Berwick
Liddel
Annan
R. Irthing
Solway Firth
Burgh – by – Sands
Carlisle
Newcastle
Hexham
grain, livestock, wool, hides, skins, fish, leather, salt, firewood, cloth, potash, wood, wine, iron, coal
Carlatton
R. Eden
Ireland
Sebergham
Castle Sowerby
Great Salkeld
Langwathby
Cockermouth
Penrith
Whitehaven
Appleby
St. Bees
Egremont
R. Kent
York
Pickering
Helmsley
Rillington
Ripon
Malton
Kendal
Borough
Scottish Border
0
25
Kilometres
0
15
Miles

properties of a small number of the leading members of Carlisle society, the Boltons for example. The remaining buildings were of wood. Some had two storeys, as can be seen in the anecdote concerning Thomas Tailor's house. In 1287 one Ralph Deblet got drunk and went upstairs into Thomas Tailor's 'solar' and fell upon Thomas who was asleep. Thomas woke up very alarmed, and Ralph fell backwards on to a cartload of wood at the bottom of the stairs. Whatever the truth of this incident, the unfortunate Thomas was hanged for murder.

The archaeological evidence for buildings in medieval Carlisle is not as full as that for the Roman period. In 1977 excavations at Castle Street revealed rectangular buildings based on stone foundations. Inside the buildings were hearths, a barrel-lined pit and numerous other features typical of medieval life. Reconstructing the history of these plots proved very difficult, especially in view of the very short time allowed for excavation. It can be shown, however, that in medieval Carlisle, as in most other towns of the period, there were plots of varying size due to the normal practice of subletting and subdivision. The plots included a variety of features including stables, granges or barns, brewhouses, yards, wells, gardens and orchards as well as domestic accommodation.

Excavations at Annetwell Street and the site of the new extension to Tullie House Museum uncovered a large number of pits and wells belonging to the backlands of properties in existence from the twelfth century onwards. These pits and wells contained fragments of pottery vessels used for cooking and pitchers and jugs for holding wine or water. This pottery, known to archaeologists as 'Red Gritty Ware', is the earliest type made locally after the Normans arrived. Some of this material was found in timber-lined wells dated by tree-ring methods to the mid-twelfth century.

Other wells were excavated in The Lanes when the old Lanes were demolished to make way for the new shopping centre in the early 1980s. In Old Grapes Lane a timber-lined well, also dated by tree-ring techniques, was in use around 1200. Elsewhere in The Lanes there was evidence for a range of small timber buildings, properties, pits, wells and yards, reflecting both domestic and craft-based activities spanning the entire period of the Middle Ages. A series of carefully spaced pits, originally lined, in Law's Lane looks a little like a tannery, as does another group of pits between Old Grapes Lane and Crown and Anchor Lane. However, the identification of these as tan pits must be regarded as provisional, especially as this unpleasant-smelling activity tended to be sited in the suburbs.

Rows of pits that may be part of an industrial complex, excavated at Law's Lane in 1981

A well, lined with oak timbers and felled between 1279 and 1297, discovered in excavations at Keay's Lane in 1978

By the late thirteenth century the main streets so familiar today – Scotch Street, English Street, Abbey Street, Fisher Street, Blackfriars Street – were all in existence, although known by different names. The street frontages were built up, with long narrow plots to the rear. The subletting of plots, especially parcels of land behind the street frontage, created the need for access and this was achieved by making narrow lanes between properties. Many lanes survived until parts of Rickergate and Scotch Street were developed in recent years, and excavations showed that many of the narrow lanes or vennels owed their origins to the Middle Ages.

The townscape would have been dominated by the priory church and the castle, and encircled by the town walls pierced by three gates. Beyond the walls, suburbs developed in Caldewgate along Bridge Street, which was then described as the street of the Flemings or *vicus Flandrensis*. It was here that some of the less pleasant crafts such as tanning were located, and crafts that required a ready supply of water, such as dyeing and milling, were located by rivers. Doubtless the suburbs straggled along the main roads as well as along the River Caldew, but there were large open spaces as well. These formed the royal demesne lands, within which the church and some lords had property and citizens were increasingly able to lease plots in the absence of any common fields.

We can form an idea of the population levels only with the greatest difficulty as no records survive for the twelfth to thirteenth centuries that provide us with any reliable information. We might imagine that the population level gradually increased and that it measured in the hundreds. To the modern eye, however, medieval Carlisle, both in terms of numbers of people and density of occupation, would appear more like a village. There were substantial open spaces, two of which were filled in the mid-thirteenth century with the arrival of the friars, but the archaeological evidence suggests that much of the land behind the street frontages was also open.

The wealthiest element in the population was the burgesses, who evolved into a more or less self-perpetuating oligarchy controlling the town's fortunes for centuries. A small number of families virtually ran the town, but the influence of few of these families was maintained at the same level for more than three generations. In the thirteenth century it was the Boltons, the Tebays and the Croftons, joined later by the Grinsdales and the Harringtons, providing the mayors, the town's members of parliament, and the most prominent merchants. Below them were the artisans and the labourers, the servants, widows and children. The majority of the townsfolk were undoubtedly of local origin, migrating into the city from villages in the immediate hinterland, such as Upperby, Stanwix and Botcherby, but occasionally others came from further afield in the county, from such places as Thursby, Aspatria, Wigton, Croglin, Dacre, Culgaith, Ousby, Egremont, Cockermouth and Furness. The sons of some of these may have been sent to school, the earliest recorded mention of which was in 1187. This school was attached to the priory, but another school was established in the Blackfriars and it came to have a very good reputation.

There were inevitably tensions and quarrels, providing much work for the courts of justice. Murder seems to have been relatively uncommon, and where it did occur it was frequently within the family, between man and wife, or between quarrelsome neighbours, but occasionally rivalries between different trades may have been the cause. In the court records of 1292–3 is the case of Richard Clement, who struck the dog of Roger, son of Martin the butcher. Roger countered by striking Richard through the heart with his sword, killing him. Other common misdemeanours involved drunkenness or transgressions of the laws governing trade. The medieval citizens of Carlisle also had their share of accidental injuries and fatalities. The three-year-old son of an artisan, a bleacher, was scalded to death when a cooking pot full of boiling water fell on him.

The most serious hazard affecting towns in the Middle Ages was fire. Carlisle was no exception, indeed it may be said to be especially vulnerable as the lack of local stone meant that nearly all the buildings were made of wood. In 1251 much of the town was destroyed by fire. The fire seems to have concentrated largely on the eastern side burning Rickergate (now Scotch Street), and probably affected the market place and the Franciscan friary. The king gave two hundred oaks from Inglewood Forest to help in the rebuilding programme and the city recovered fairly quickly.

On 19 May 1292 young Simon of Orton, disinherited by Simon his father, set fire to the family property in Carlisle. It turned into a major disaster, as fire destroyed much of the walled town and spread into the suburbs beyond. The cathedral, the castle bridge, the Franciscan friary and possibly parts of the Dominican friary, together with houses, orchards and warehouses, were burnt. Evidence that the fire may have affected the Dominican friary as well was recovered in the excavations at Blackfriars Street. Here parts of the church, if not the whole building, was reconstructed from the foundations up. A number of oak piles providing support for the foundations were found. They were dated by tree-ring methods, which showed that the trees from which the piles were made were felled some time between 1284 and 1302. Altogether, some nine lives were lost in this great fire and much property was looted. Simon, the culprit, was sentenced to be hanged for homicide and burnt for arson.

War and Pestilence

Towns in the Middle Ages could and did recover from the effects of fire fairly quickly, but Carlisle suffered more than one misfortune after 1292 that affected its ability to recover. The city was placed under direct royal control; it had a sheriff, William of Mulcastre, who dealt particularly harshly with alleged abuses by the leading citizens. The Anglo-Scottish wars commenced in 1296, and in 1303 another serious fire destroyed the newly rebuilt Rickergate and part of Botchergate (now English Street). As if that were not enough, further calamities took place in the second decade of the century and the wars continued.

The threat of war had been building up for some time, and in late March 1296 the Earl of Buchan arrived at Carlisle after ravaging Arthuret and Nicholforest. The people of Carlisle were taken by surprise. Fishermen in the Eden were killed, mills and suburbs burnt. A fire was started within the city by a Scottish prisoner and conflagration followed. The Scots attacked too quickly, however, and they were unable to consolidate their position without the aid of siege engines. The following day they withdrew. In 1297 William Wallace, one of the most renowned Scottish leaders, led another attack, but this too was repulsed.

For just over ten years from the outbreak of war, Carlisle became a focal point in the governance of England. By 1298 the king, Edward I, had placed English soldiers on the Solway to counter further attacks, and for the next three years English armies mustered at Carlisle for attacks into Scotland. The impact on Carlisle must have been enormous. The population swelled to unprecedented proportions with the presence of the armies. The meadows and fields, formerly a lucrative source of income to the sheriff and bishop, yielded none at all in some years, so devastated were they by the horses and the needs of the soldiers. An even greater impact was felt when the king himself visited the town, as happened on several occasions. In 1307 Edward summoned the Parliament to attend him at Carlisle. The Prince of Wales, 10 earls, 76 barons, at least 68 senior clerics and some 248 knights arrived. Together with their retinues, for medieval magnates never travelled alone, one estimate suggested that there were at least two thousand extra people to feed and house. This colossal strain on resources lasted for several weeks, and all these magnates had to wait as the king was too ill be moved from his bed at Lanercost Priory, where some two hundred retainers attended him. By the early summer Edward was sufficiently recovered to travel on horseback and resume his campaigns in Scotland. He rode along what is now Caldewgate and Newtown Road, through Kirkandrews on Eden to Burgh by Sands. It was here that he died on 7 July.

There were other disadvantages in having such a large presence of outsiders in Carlisle. Young bloods were able to run riot, and caused much damage. Prominent among them was Prince Edward, who had to compensate Joan of Botcherby for the damage caused to her croft and garden. The prince with his retinue, including dogs, hawks and a lion, seems also to have burnt Wetheral Priory. It is easy to imagine the relief when the army moved on.

On the other hand there were many distinct advantages. During the Parliament's sojourn, substantial sums were offered up at church altars. Building work was put in hand, at the king and queen's expense, in the Keep and other Inner Ward buildings in the castle, at the cathedral and at the Dominican friary. The king's household

Lanercost Priory seen through the arch of the ruined gatehouse. King Edward I spent many weeks here during his final illness in 1307

expenditure in Carlisle amounted to £2,895, a sum beyond the wildest dreams of the citizens. Huge stocks of food and drink for the royal household would have entered the city from other parts of the country. The benefits to the tradesmen in servicing and supplying the retainers were probably greater than at any other time, and the town centre would have been extremely busy as soldiers, knights, and great lords went about their business, and took part in ceremonies and religious processions.

The death of Edward I marked a temporary cessation in hostilities for a short time. This allowed Robert Bruce to regain the initiative, and in 1311 he ravaged parts of northern Cumbria. Tribute was collected in order to mollify Bruce, but this peace was not to last, for in 1314 he established himself at Rose Castle, from where he directed the ravaging of much of the county. He made a desultory attack on the city in that year, but it was in 1315 that the harrying began in earnest. Carlisle was prepared and the commander, Andrew de Harcla, mustered over five hundred archers, knights, hobelars and men-at-arms against an expected attack. The siege lasted ten days, during which Bruce brought up ladders for scaling the walls, siege engines,

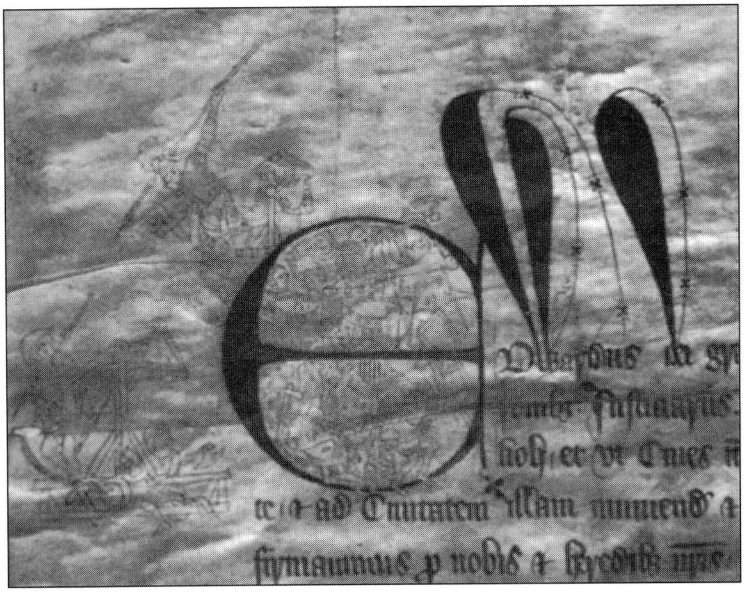

The initial letter of the royal charter of 1316 has been decorated with scenes showing the siege of Sir Andrew de Harcla in 1315

and substantial numbers of soldiers and miners for undermining the city walls. Bruce himself was stationed next to the Church of the Holy Trinity in Caldewgate, while his men attacked the gates and walls on all sides. The whole effort took place in torrential rain and proved disastrous for Bruce. He failed to capture the town, and his siege engines, including a great tower, became bogged down in the quagmires.

The city defences, however, especially those of the castle, were often in a poor state of repair. In 1321 we learn that part of the curtain walls were in a state of collapse; 'wall 40 feet long collapsed and another 120 feet long about to collapse in outer bailey near Caldew Bridge'. Demolition was needed and new buttresses were required for the rebuilt wall. This work followed earlier repairs of 33 roods in length in 1303, and further repairs to a breech made near the postern in 1308.

Throughout the fourteenth century the Scots continued their attacks on Cumbria, destroying the countryside, burning crops and houses, and looting. In 1316 the Scots killed and pillaged in the east of the county, down the Eden Valley and ended up around Penrith. Some of these raids were so devastating as to render whole communities valueless, especially in the north of the county. The disruption this caused was incalculable, and was made even worse by a series of bad summers, disastrous harvests, and diseases affecting cattle. There were

Map of Cumbria showing the places raided by Bruce between 1316 and 1322

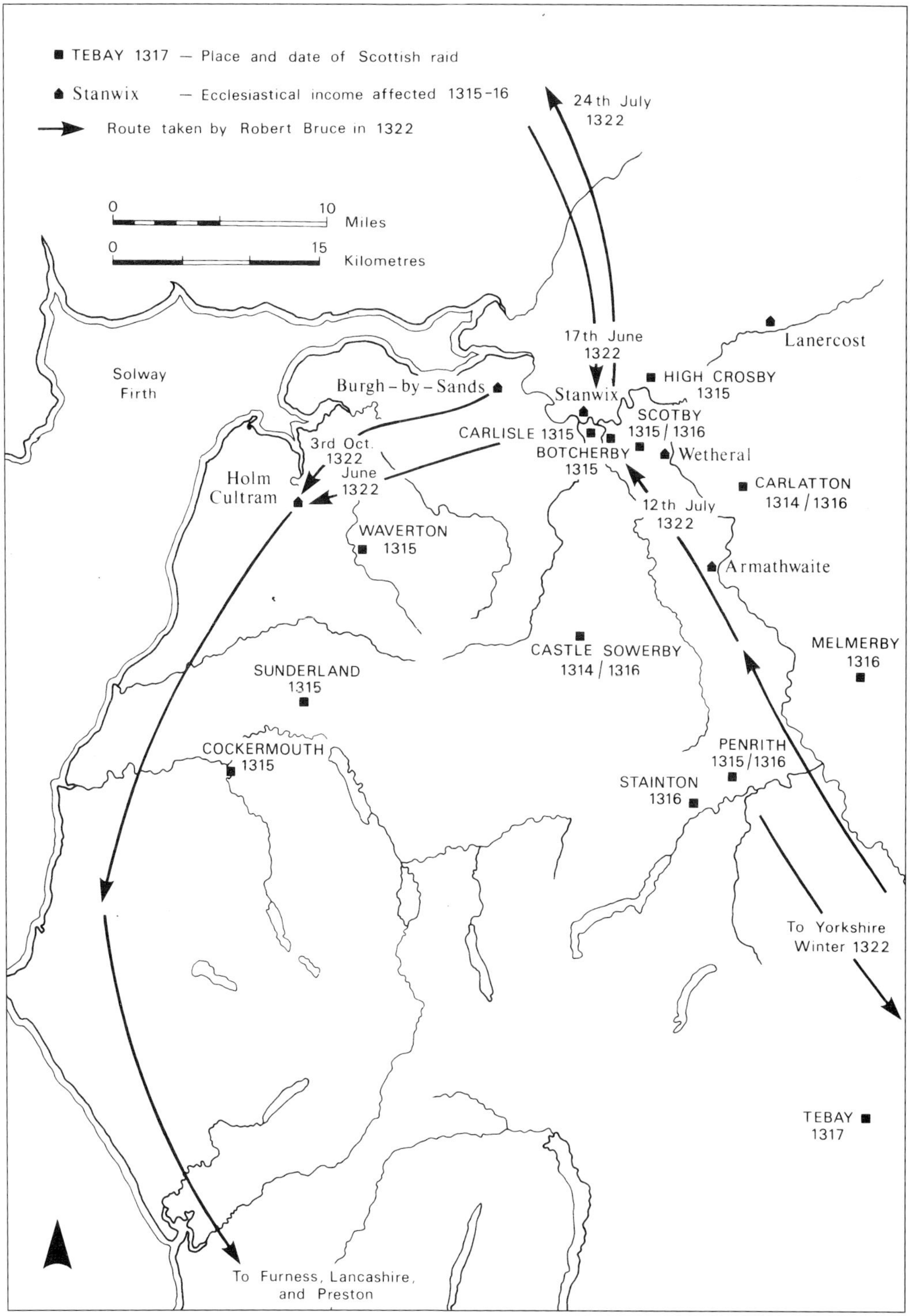
TEBAY 1317 — Place and date of Scottish raid
Stanwix — Ecclesiastical income affected 1315-16
Route taken by Robert Bruce in 1322
0 10 Miles
0 15 Kilometres
24th July 1322
Solway Firth
17th June 1322
Lanercost
HIGH CROSBY 1315
Burgh-by-Sands
Stanwix
SCOTBY 1315/1316
CARLISLE 1315
3rd Oct. 1322
BOTCHERBY 1315
Wetheral
Holm Cultram
June 1322
CARLATTON 1314/1316
12th July 1322
WAVERTON 1315
Armathwaite
MELMERBY 1316
CASTLE SOWERBY 1314/1316
SUNDERLAND 1315
PENRITH 1315/1316
COCKERMOUTH 1315
STAINTON 1316
To Yorkshire Winter 1322
TEBAY 1317
To Furness, Lancashire, and Preston

truces, but they mostly failed and the Scots returned. In 1345, for example, there were two attacks. The first, in May, destroyed much of the barony of Greystoke, near Penrith. The second attack, led by King David II in October, bypassed Carlisle but destroyed Stanwix, and then left much of the Eden Valley in flames. Castle Carrock, Cumrew, Croglin, Renwick, Kirkoswald, Lazonby, Great Salkeld and Penrith were ruined. The impact on Carlisle and its hinterland was devastating. A contemporary description captures the mood well. Its air was 'so corrupted and tainted by dung and manure heaps and much other filth put in the streets and lanes that the men dwelling there and coming to the city for its defence are stricken with a dreadful horror'. Violence and disorder became endemic. When Allen Gunson threw his goods and chattels into the street from his house, which was on fire, his neighbours, instead of looking after them, ran off with as much as they could carry. On another occasion Alice, wife of Sir Thomas Lengleys, was less afraid of the Scots than of her husband, who had scalped and beaten her and made her miscarry, as well as breaking the back of a child.

Such matters were not confined to the general public. Clerics were not immune to quarrelling between themselves and were even, on occasion, violent. In the 1380s the canons were bitterly divided over the election of a new prior. Allegations of incompetence, negligence, violence, adultery and even incontinence abounded. The new prior, Thomas Dalston, unwilling to let matters rest and continually feuding, was eventually excommunicated by the bishop, and this led to both clergy and citizens indulging in what was almost a riot. Order was eventually restored and Dalston resigned shortly afterwards.

The threat of war and violence, not to mention harvest failures, was a fact of life throughout much of the century. Tensions between the townsfolk and the soldiers in the castle, led by Bishop Kirkby who was also the constable of the castle, resulted in mayhem on Sunday, 31 July 1345. During a performance of a miracle play in the market place two men, one of them a servant of the bishop, quarrelled. Another of the bishop's servants intervened, whereupon a local magnate, Peter de Tilliol, whose servant was the man involved, sent for the bishop. Bishop Kirkby replied by sending a force of thirty-one armed men to the scene, where by this time the mayor and bailiffs had gathered to look into the matter. The soldiers loosed off a volley of arrows, killing one bystander, and then went on the rampage, shooting arrows into every open window. Both incensed and terrified, the mayor and bailiffs sent a deputation to the castle to arrest the culprits, but the garrison retaliated by carrying out an assault on the townsfolk.

They went down Castle Street towards the cathedral shooting, beating and generally running amok. Eventually the garrison withdrew back into the castle, leaving the townspeople frightened at what might happen next. In fact the trouble gradually subsided, doubtless in the face of further Scottish attacks, the second of which came in October 1345.

Other trouble was to come. In the autumn of 1349 the Black Death arrived in the county. The exact impact is hard to quantify. The sheriff found great difficulty in raising revenues from 'divers lands which after that plague, to wit, for a whole year and a half remained untilled for lack of workers'. Estimates of the numbers of deaths vary, but they could have been as high as one-third to two-thirds the population, while even higher proportions may have died in Stanwix and elsewhere. Nor was this the only visitation of the plague. Further pestilencies occurred in almost every decade throughout the rest of the century, in 1361–2, 1369, 1379–80 and 1391. In 1362 William de Fenton left his goods and chattels in his tenement in Castle Street to his wife and two children 'if they live'. If any should die 'in the present mortality let the survivors have them'.

It was not just war and plague that contributed to the depopulation of the town. Another development was the imposition by the king of the poll tax, which was levied for three years in 1377, 1379 and 1381. The returns for 1377 list 678 names, but this clearly does not account for everybody as recent experience demonstrates. By comparing the returns for each of the three years, it is possible to identify some of the people who went missing. John of Fournes, a smith, was listed as the tenant of a property in Caldewgate in 1379, but not in 1377. Wealthy residents such as Peter de Gaytone, who was robbed of 40s. of gold in 1384, went unrecorded in the poll tax returns. Others were not required to pay the tax, including those who were very poor and vagrants, children and the clergy.

Finally, to cap a century of almost unmitigated disaster, came one more. On 4 May 1391 there was another devastating fire. It destroyed about three-quarters of the city, including the market place, Rickergate (Scotch Street), Botchergate (English Street), Castle Street, St Cuthbert's church and around 1,500 homes.

The End of the Middle Ages

The opening of a new century did nothing to lessen the fear of war. To some extent this had been anticipated earlier at the castle, where major alterations took place over several years from 1378. The Outer

Gatehouse, de Ireby's Tower, was substantially rebuilt by John Lewyn, one of the principal military architects of his day. He turned the original gatehouse, which was probably severely functional, into something more akin to a residence for the constable of the castle. Incorporated in it were prisons, including an underground dungeon, a kitchen, a service area, a solar and hall, together with other ground-floor rooms presumably given over to a steward and gaoler. Provision was made for fireplaces and toilets, the latter accommodated within the thickness of the walls.

The building accounts for much of this work survive, and show how the work was organized. Masons were recruited, and barrows, spades, shovels, iron wedges, ropes and other tools were bought. Stone was quarried at Blackhall and Unthank, and timber for posts, boards, laths, piles and planks was trimmed on the spot in Inglewood Forest. Sand and lime, from Caldewstones and Bolton Fell respectively, were needed for mortar, and lead for roofing came from Wensleydale. Large numbers of people were required for transporting the materials and doing the building work and not all were of local extraction, for Lewyn brought with him craftsmen with whom he had worked on other projects. All had to be paid and fed. Much of the work was seasonal, however, commencing in May and stopping in the winter. Other building works were also put in hand in the castle. The Inner Gatehouse, known as the Captain's Tower, was enlarged and decorated with tracery that can still be seen. The 'New Tower' was re-roofed and a great many other minor buildings, which no longer survive, would have been required, if only to service the craftsmen working on the Outer Gatehouse.

A fragment of a funerary monument probably dating to the fifteenth century found incorporated into the wall of a building in Old Bush Lane

Throughout this period the church continued to play its part. Work on the fabric of the priory, following the destruction wrought by the fire of 1292 over a hundred years earlier, had still not been completed. One of the events at the cathedral must have been the installation of the great east window, possibly in 1359, during a burst of activity extending over a decade from 1354. This was followed over half a century later by the completion of the north transept, the tower and crossing before Bishop Strickland's death in 1419. In the middle of the fifteenth century the magnificent choir stalls were installed.

St Alban's church was also still in use. In 1356 a commission was appointed to look into its status. It found that, although services had been performed and burials made there for generations past, the church did not appear to have been consecrated. The bishop accordingly temporarily suspended all services and, despite the occasional gift, such as that of money for a bell and glazing half a window in 1395, by the end of the fourteenth century St Alban's church was probably equivalent in status to a chantry chapel.

Trade was also heavily disrupted but it continued. Many people whose occupations are recorded were connected in some way with the textile trade, weavers, fullers, tailors, dyers, and a blanket maker. Archaeology rarely produces much in the way of direct evidence of textiles, although wool and cloth were England's principal industries, but excavations at the Cumberland Building Society headquarters in Castle Street yielded several small fragments of medium and coarse cloth. They include twills, one of which had traces of a stripe dyed with madder. Not all the fragments had been fulled, suggesting perhaps that the cloth had been woven in a domestic context. An exceptional fragment appears to be of camel hair, an unusual testament to the widespread trade networks enjoyed by many English towns. The same excavation also produced many fragments of shoes, while the leather offcuts, found here and in a pit in Castle Street itself, show that leather working was taking place. This is not surprising for, as we have seen earlier in the Middle Ages, the leather trades were probably the second most important in Carlisle.

Other occupations are also attested. A John Fletcher and Robert Lorimer made arrows and spurs, while Thomas Bladesmith may have been a cutler. In 1384–5 Richard Potter, a name that suggests he may have made metal pots, was paid 26s. 8d. for casting three bronze guns, the earliest reference to this kind of firepower in Carlisle. No earthenware potters are mentioned in the written sources but local production in pottery kilns is likely, at least for the twelfth and thirteenth centuries. By the late fourteenth and fifteenth centuries, however, the reduced green-glazed jugs so typical of the time may have been imported into the city from kilns located elsewhere.

Trade was maintained with Ireland and with other towns in northern England. Robert Karlell, probably the town's MP, was master of a small ship known as *La Clement* of York, and traded by sea between the east and west coasts. Trade with Scotland was also maintained despite the frequent prohibitions made by both the English and Scottish governments. Much of this trade was unexceptional, involving the same range of goods as in the thirteenth century. It was undertaken on a regular basis, but it was rarely on a large scale and traders did not necessarily specialize in any one commodity. For example, in 1412 a Scottish chapman, Gilbert del Chambre, brought to Carlisle a single broadcloth and some boots. A few weeks later he was back with forty beasts, probably cattle, leaving with cards, boots and shoes. The following year he was exporting more cloth and leatherwork as well as knives.

Troubles with the Scots continued into the fifteenth century, and the additions and modernization made to the Outer Gatehouse from 1378 onwards were certainly needed. Following Henry IV's expedition to Scotland in 1400, Carlisle and the borders were once more vulnerable. It is no wonder, after the events of the previous century, that in 1401 the citizens of Carlisle were on the point of leaving on account of the raids by the Scots. In 1402 the king said that a Scottish force 'had been in our kingdom near our vill of Carlisle in number around 12,000 and had done what evil they could, but praised be our lord this was but little'. Further problems followed, exacerbated by the rebellion of the Percies, Earls of Northumberland, against the king. The defences were in a poor state of repair, as the citizens said in 1409 'lately the gates and a great part of the walls have fallen to the ground', and trade with Scotland was badly affected. In the reign of Henry V, further raiding by the Scots disrupted life in Cumberland, while occasional English forays penetrated the Scottish borders. All this was related to the king's campaigns against the French, whose allies the Scots were. The extent of the destruction is difficult to quantify, but many religious houses, Carlisle Priory among them, received tax exemptions. A truce was finally agreed upon in 1424, and this was followed by nearly a generation of relative peace, although at the level of the nobility there was plenty of quarrelling.

Peace was very welcome, for in the 1430s a combination of plague, bad weather leading to flooding, the loss of cattle through disease, and poor harvests once again reduced parts of the population in Cumbria to its knees. Population levels may have continued to fall, and vacant sites in the suburbs and within the city walls are known in Annetwell Street, Abbey Street, Botchergate (English Street), and Fisher Street. Further evidence can be found in the low valuations attached to the castle demesne lands and to the falling revenues from the local estates of the Percies, Earls of Northumberland.

Further troubles with the Scots surfaced again in the 1440s and 1450s, and this led to full-scale war between England and Scotland in 1456. Carlisle suffered in this conflict, which was as much between the Lancastrians and Yorkists as it was about old rivalries with the Scots. In 1461 Queen Margaret, in addition to promising to cede Berwick to the Scots, also promised to give Carlisle to them in return for their assistance in capturing it. Upperby and the suburb of Caldcotes were destroyed, as well as the city's mills and gates. The besiegers seem to have broken into the city and caused great

Carvings made by prisoners held in the Keep at Carlisle Castle in the fifteenth century

destruction, including the Tithe Barn, but it was eventually relieved through the efforts of Richard Salkeld.

In the sixteenth century two significant events took place that permanently altered the appearance of the city. The Dissolution of the Monasteries by Henry VIII resulted in the destruction of the two friaries. The same king's fear of invasion by the Scots led him to construct fortifications in many places. In Carlisle this included works at the castle and at the Botchergate, an area known today as the Courts.

Carlisle Priory was a long-established institution. It was headed by the prior, and under him was a subprior who may have doubled up as the cellarer; a pittancer provided additions to the diet of the canons, of whom there were about fifteen; financial control was in the hands of the bursar, while the elderly and infirm would have been cared for by the master of the infirmary; a sacristan looked after the fabric of the buildings; music and liturgy were catered for by the precentor and succentor. There were a number of other officials, some of whom, like the steward, were members of the laity.

The canons received their income from various estates granted to them over the centuries. They had granges at Newbiggin, Harraby and Newlaithes, while small sums were obtained from Ainstable, Cargo and Crofton; there were in all some ninety-one places, mostly in Cumberland but some in Westmorland and Northumberland. In Carlisle, the priory owned at least 113 properties within the walls as well as others in Caldewgate, Shaddongate and Weryholme. The income from these properties, as well as tithes, went towards the canons' upkeep. They had a number of servants who ministered to their daily wants, including a doorkeeper, a butler, a cook and subcook, a brewer and a maltster, a carpenter, a tiler, a candlemaker, a laundress and a privy cleaner.

By the time of the Dissolution the canons had long since renounced the rather more austere life that governed their order when they first arrived in Carlisle over four hundred years earlier. They occupied their own rooms and the prior lived in what is now known as the Prior's Tower, with its fine ceiling painted in the time of Simon Senhouse. They had a varied diet, eating a great deal of fish, including white and red herrings and salmon, as well as oxen, sheep, piglets and geese. Their food was highly seasoned with caraway, ginger, pepper, mustard, sugar, raisins and almonds, and they drank red and spiced wines with comfets (sweets) and biscuits.

The life of the cathedral revolved around the daily acts of worship. At the centre was the statue of the Virgin and the high altar. The church was richly decorated with a red and green roof, while the choir piers were painted white with red roses in a diaper pattern. The backs of the choir stalls were painted with scenes from the life of various saints including St Cuthbert, which still survive. The altar cloths, vestments and silver plate added to the splendour, which was completed by the sound of the choristers singing the Mass.

By contrast with the priory, the numbers of friars had fallen significantly by the time of the Dissolution. By 1534 there were only four Dominican friars (Blackfriars) and nine Franciscans (Greyfriars). The Blackfriars had a church with a leaded roof and two bells, a 'stone house', which may have been domestic, a kiln house, and a refectory with a chamber outside and store-rooms above. A map of Carlisle drawn in the middle of the century appears to show a double cloister. This seems a little excessive for the friars at Carlisle, not to mention the difficulty there must have been in squeezing two cloistral ranges into the tight space between Blackfriars Street and West Walls.

The curates of St Mary's and St Cuthbert's churches probably also said masses for the departed at chantry chapels, of which there were five in Carlisle. One of these was in St Alban's church, and all were dissolved shortly after the friaries and the priory. The Reformation in Carlisle began with the arrival of the king's commissioners on 9 January 1541. They dissolved the priory the same day and began to put their other instructions into effect at the same time. Some of the canons were pensioned off but others remained, and the administration was transferred to the new Dean and Chapter.

During this period, up to the Reformation of Henry VIII, the city's defences had been a perpetual worry and drain on expenses. While the crown had an interest in ensuring that Carlisle was adequately protected, the citizens were never quite sure how much of the burden of maintenance should fall to them. The king made periodic murage grants for the walls and gates, but such payments were often inadequate. In the 1340s, for example, it was reported that 'parts of the walls are ruinous for want of repair', and in 1347 one stretch was in danger of imminent collapse. Between 1422 and 1426 some £286 16s. 8¾d. was spent on the defences of the castle and city walls. Another £80 had to be spent in December 1426, and by December 1429, less than three years after the previous outlay, the gates and walls of the city were said to be 'so ruinous and defective that if any hostile incursion were made, the city would probably be lost'. The defences were improved. Not only were the Botchergate and the Rickergate restored and improved, but the city had its own guns and ammunition in the form of 543 gunstones and saltpetre, and received large numbers of longbows, bowstrings, arrows, and other armaments.

By the late 1530s work on the defences was once again imperative, this time with the threat of war from France and Scotland as the catalyst. Henry VIII put in hand a national programme of defence refurbishment, and this included Carlisle, where a Bohemian land surveyor and engineer, Stefan von Haschenperg, was put in charge. Work was concentrated on the castle and the former Botchergate, which was turned into a citadel.

At the castle Haschenperg strengthened the wall dividing the inner from the outer ward by providing the wall walk with the necessary space for cannon, and he added the half-moon battery. The keep was also strengthened with merlons and embrasures for cannon. Outside the east wall, in the area now occupied by the children's playground in Bitts Park, Haschenperg added substantial outworks. All in all the plan here was to prevent attackers getting anywhere near the actual walls of the castle and the inner ward. Indeed, the latter was turned into a castle within the castle. At the Botchergate Haschenperg's plans entailed the elimination of the old medieval point of entry and the building of a new citadel based around two large drum towers with a central range, which probably incorporated the older medieval work, the whole tied together by curtain walls and ditches. A new gate, known as the Newgate, was inserted towards the southern end of the West Walls. Excavations here in 1978 revealed slight traces of this gate, but most

An engraving by Luke Clennel in 1813 showing the Captain's Tower and Half Moon Battery at Carlisle Castle

of the remains had been removed when the new County Gaol was built in 1824–7.

These massive works relied partly upon firepower for their effectiveness, but the necessary ordnance was slow to arrive. By 1545 the citadel still had no guns, while the city and the castle could only boast one aged gunner between them. The citizens were so incensed at the crown's tardiness that they offered to restore the city's defences themselves. This they did, with the crown's consent, and thus made some of the new works redundant before building had been completed. Haschenperg was dismissed for incompetence in 1543, but the real blame undoubtedly lay with the king who, despite the warnings he issued in the early 1540s against the danger of Scottish attack, failed to provide the ordnance needed, although by way of pacification a force of 500–600 men was considered as an alternative. The Scots did invade, but were repulsed at the battle of Solway Moss in November 1542. War continued until peace was made in 1550, by which time the city's defences were in such a parlous condition that several lengths of city wall had collapsed in the previous year.

An aerial view of Carlisle from the south-east showing the circular towers first built by Henry VIII's incompetent surveyor, Stefan von Haschenperg, in about 1542

During the first half of the sixteenth century, in common with the national trend, there are indications that the population levels in Cumberland were rising, although the increases would appear to be very small by twentieth-century standards. Estimates based on the main sources, the 1377 poll tax returns and the 1534 muster-roll, suggest that numbers may have risen from about 1,500 to 1,700, an increase of about 200, but even this brought with it difficulties in feeding. The soils of northern Cumbria, however they are assessed, were never the most productive for cereal crops, and there are very large areas of poorly drained boulder clays fit only for woodland or grazing.

As in previous centuries, the people of Carlisle, apart from the clergy and military, relied on trade for their livelihood to a considerable extent. Carlisle's hinterland continued to include not just northern Cumberland but Scotland as well, wars, feuding, and plain dislike of one another, notwithstanding. In 1534 Agnes Carodders of Dalston was charged with harbouring 'vagabonds and Scots', as though the terms were synonymous. Scots, nevertheless, continued to move south, often as servants, sometimes as refugees, taking no notice of any cross-border restrictions there may have been. After 1482 Carlisle and Berwick were the only two places in northern England that the Scots could lawfully trade with. Many of the wares traded were the same as in centuries past, but there were also bridles, saddles, steel bonnets, spurs, stirrups, linen, wine and salt. Indeed, a portion of Carlisle's wine supply came from France, redistributed through the ports of south-west Scotland, while its fish, despite the excellence of the local supplies as noted by William Camden, seems to have come almost entirely from Scotland.

Trade with Ireland may have fallen away by the sixteenth century, for there is little evidence that the ports and creeks around Whitehaven, Skinburness, Maryport and Boustead Hill, near Burgh by Sands, were utilized as fully as they could have been. Contacts with London and the south were maintained, however, as was necessary in fiscal, political and military terms. Men of Carlisle, Kendal and Penrith are variously recorded at Coventry, Southampton, London as well as Newcastle, York, Berwick and Hull. It was Newcastle, however, with which the citizens of Carlisle had the most contact. Newcastle had preferential rates for the export of wool and lead, and was a key redistributive centre for northern England generally. In 1515, for example, a Thomas Denton bought quantities of sheep skins in Carlisle and took them to Newcastle for sale. Being unable to sell them there he took them overseas on a Dutch ship, sold them, and returned with a load of iron that he sold in Carlisle. Trade in wine, iron, skins and many other goods, together with institutional links, such as that of the prior of Carlisle with St Nicholas, Newcastle, and doubtless family considerations, linked Carlisle with Newcastle at most levels of society.

York, too, was a key focus of life for the citizens of Carlisle, partly because it was the ecclesiastical capital and administrative centre of northern England, but also because it was, with Hull, one of the principal commercial centres in the north. Indeed, a substantial number of York's immigrants and freemen were of Cumbrian, if not Carlisle, extraction.

Carlisle's trade with its own immediate hinterland provided the mainstay of its prosperity. The lists of items bought and sold is very long, dominated by a variety of cloths including felts, kerseys, linen, broadcloth, fustian, muslins, worsteds and many more, in a variety of colours. Crops and animal products also figured highly, as they did in almost every other town at the time. Agricultural products provided employment for many craftsmen: tanners, glovers, weavers, cordwainers and butchers, bakers, cooks and brewers. Weaponry and domestic utensils, including bronze pots, candlesticks, knives and many other items, were made by potters, armourers, jack-makers, goldsmiths and glaziers, among others.

Trade in the towns of medieval England had always been regulated by the guilds, but evidence for the conduct of trade in Carlisle survives only from the fifteenth century. In 1561, however, the mayor, Robert

Dalton, together with the weavers, glovers, shoemakers and tailors, codified the regulations in what has become known as the Dormont Book. Whereas in earlier centuries Carlisle was governed by a small group of wealthy merchants, from 1561 craftsmen for the first time acquired a voice. This led to bitter disputes between the mayor, previous mayors, the craftsmen and other members of the ruling oligarchy. Although Dalton eventually lost his franchise and government reverted to the wealthy classes, the craftsmen retained their place in the conduct of civic affairs.

The city oligarchy, the Aglionbys, the Blennerhassets, the Skeltons, for example, many of whom had connections with magnates such as the Dacres or Nevilles, owed their wealth in most instances to the cloth trade, but many also had substantial properties in Carlisle. One, a lawyer named John Middleton, at the end of Elizabeth's reign owned twenty-six burgages in the city as well as much outside. The acquisition of property was seen not only as an investment but as a key to their social standing.

Such families represented a small proportion of the population, which was otherwise made up of landless wage-earners and those professional men who were leaders in their trades but not members of the ruling élite. At the lower end of the scale were many artisans and shopkeepers. Some were sufficiently well off to afford a servant and even weapons and, like the servants and labourers at the bottom of the social heap, supplemented their incomes with other employment.

A view of Carlisle in the reign of Elizabeth is preserved in a map probably drawn in the 1560s, and now in the British Library. It shows only the walled area, omitting the suburbs. It is difficult to be certain about how much confidence should be placed in the map as a whole, for although some details have a genuine look, nevertheless the way in which many buildings are depicted, and the omission of some of the vennels known from other sources to have been present in The Lanes area, for example, suggest that it is a stylized representation, seen from a bird's-eye view. Even so, the pattern of main streets is instantly recognizable as that of the present day, and the appearance of a town with large open spaces, gardens and orchards, is certainly accurate as the observations of John Leland, the King's Antiquary, in the 1530s bear witness. In other words, if one left the city walls out of account, Carlisle in the reign of Elizabeth would have resembled what to modern eyes would be a village.

The streets themselves would have been unmetalled, and in winter passage would doubtless have been made more difficult with mud and potholes. In the town centre was the market square with its pillory, the

Carlesle
Every inch contayneth one hundreth foote

The earliest map of Carlisle made about 1560 is in the British Library

market cross, the grain and malt markets, the shambles (meat market) containing some twenty-six stalls, a fish market, the Moot Hall and Redness Hall, now the Guildhall Museum. The market place, with the nearby cathedral precinct and St Cuthbert's church, was the social and economic centre of town life. At the southern end stood the imposing, if somewhat redundant, citadel, while the north end was dominated by the castle, whose forbidding bulk was alleviated in the 1570s by Lord Scrope's modernization of what became known as the Elizabethan range, in one corner of which Mary Queen of Scots was temporarily housed in 1568.

Although the population was gradually increasing, it had not reached the point at which there was any pressure on space. The Greyfriars site was still vacant nearly twenty years after the Dissolution, and if the map is any guide, the amount of unbuilt-on land behind the street frontages was considerable, not to mention the occasional frontage site in use as a garden.

The only substantial buildings at this date, as in earlier times, were the castle, the churches, the Moot Hall and the occasional stone house.

The Guildhall, a building erected in the mid-fourteenth century and later extended and modified at the end of the century

Most of the buildings were of timber and, according to the map, the majority were single-storey only. It is unlikely that this was strictly the case, however, as there are instances where descriptions of buildings clearly show the presence of first floors and it is in these that brightly coloured wall hangings contributed to both the warmth and decoration of the rooms. We can only hazard a guess as to the appearance of cottages occupied by the artisans and labourers, but Celia Fiennes' mention of single-storeyed buildings of wood, clay and thatch in the 1690s is probably a fair reflection of the situation.

The wealthier classes occupied somewhat more opulent surroundings, as can be seen from the surviving wills. When Richard Blennerhasset died in 1571, an inventory of his goods refers to a buttery, kitchen, larder house, brewing house, presser chamber, a hall, a high chamber, a low chamber, a chapel chamber, a servants' chamber, a stable and a garden. This may not have been typical, for we hear of other prominent citizens who had smaller premises, containing a loft, a hall, three chambers, a little closet and a kitchen. The house of Anthony Rumney also contained a children's chamber.

The most important house in sixteenth-century Carlisle, and probably the largest, was the White Hall, now known as Tullie House. The inventory of Sir Thomas Dacre of Lanercost, who died there in 1575, shows it to have consisted of an inner chamber, a closet, a new hall, a lady's bedchamber, a maid's chamber, a new buttery, an old inner chamber, an old outer chamber, an old kitchen, a new kitchen, a dry larder and an old buttery. Together with the gold and silver plate, the jewels, table cloths, silk and woollen clothes, the furnishings and fittings, this house must have been the ultimate in luxury to which the city's ruling élite aspired.

CHAPTER FOUR

The Emergence of the Modern City of Carlisle

The Late Sixteenth to the Eighteenth Centuries

Although Carlisle during the reign of Elizabeth and her successor, James I, was a relatively peaceful place, the inhabitants were rarely able to forget the crucial position they occupied on the border with Scotland. In 1568 the threat of trouble once more came to the fore when Elizabeth's Catholic sister, Mary Queen of Scots, was in residence in the castle. Although she was not exactly held prisoner, nevertheless, she was kept under very close supervision in what became known as Queen Mary's Tower, lest she escape and form a focus for the simmering resentments of the northern Catholic nobles. Many of her servants and retinue were ensconced in the city, and her guardians, Sir Francis Knollys and Lord Scrope, were anxious for Mary to be moved further away before her supporters attempted a rescue. This would not have been difficult. The now familiar story of the castle in a state of decay had been highlighted only three years earlier, when a survey of the castle drew attention to the unrepaired breach some 70 feet long in the wall of the outer bailey, 'through which breach men may easily pass and repass'. The keep, too, was in a state of collapse following an explosion some years earlier, while the castle's ordnance was in a sorry state.

Some work was done, partly at Scrope's own expense, and the garrison was enhanced to the point of deterring the Dacres – who were among the leading Catholic families in the north and a focus for the pro-Mary faction – from attempting any rash move. Even so, it was not enough and the castle languished for want of maintenance for the rest of the century. It is no wonder that the Duke of Buccleuch was

An inscription showing Lord Scrope's work at the castle. Below the date 1577 the inscription reads (in translation): 'Queen Elizabeth erected this work at her own expense while Lord Scrope was Warden of the Western Marches'

able, by means of a smash-and-grab raid, to rescue the border reiver, William Armstrong of Kinmont (Kinmont Willie), in a daring night raid on 13 April 1596. Armstrong had been captured on a day of truce (17 March) and was therefore immune from arrest at that time. So successful was the raid that the men on watch were unaware that it was taking place until it was almost over. The ineffectiveness of the castle guard was commented upon a year later, when a report stated that when a gun had to be fired to raise the alarm, nobody in the castle knew how to use the ordnance. On this occasion they were saved by a quick-thinking visitor from Berwick who knew what to do! In 1605 a number of thieves, incarcerated in the castle gaol, escaped simply by walking out when the servants bringing their supper forgot to close the door. Shortly afterwards, probably around 1611, the gaol was transferred to the citadel.

The defences of the castle and city continued to decay in the early years of the seventeenth century. During this time the contemporary view of the castle changed from being a focus of arms against border conflict, to being a residence for the Lord Warden of the March, and later for members of the Border Commissioners who took over when the Wardenship was abolished in 1605. By the 1630s the defences were weakened still further when the only serviceable cannon the city and castle had between them was removed first to Berwick, and then to the Tower of London.

This was unfortunate because in 1638 the Scots, antagonized by the king's tactlessness, were once again threatening war. By April 1639 the garrison had been strengthened by the addition of 500 Irish soldiers, and a further 300 sent by Lord Clifford and others. Sir Francis Willoughby, commander of the Irish forces, who saw Carlisle as 'a place of some importance', set to work restoring the castle and citadel. Not only was its defensive potential greatly improved, but Carlisle's function as a base for operating widely over the region was appreciated. Willoughby reported that every space within the castle and in the city, including the cathedral, was examined with a view to storing grain and baking bread.

In 1641 the Scots eventually arrived and were bought off with the disbandment of the Carlisle garrison, but few of the people in the north believed that the peace would last. In the following two years many of the king's sympathizers in the county were dispersed, but Carlisle was left as a Royalist island until after the crucial battle of Marston Moor in 1644. Subsequently, stocks were laid in readiness for a siege by Sir Thomas Glemham, and in October of that year the Scots began their siege. Mills and suburbs were destroyed, and doubtless the walls took a pounding from the Scots cannon, but according to an eyewitness, the young Isaac Tullie, they did not attempt a full-scale attack.

The city was ringed with batteries, the Scots to the north and west at Murrell Hill, Newtown, Caldcotes, Etterby and Stanwix, the English to the south and east at the Swifts, Fusehill, Harraby and St Nicholas. Almost nothing is known of these siege-works, and in some cases they may have consisted of little more than an emplacement for guns. In other cases, as at St Nicholas, which survived into the early eighteenth century, they were formidable star-shaped redoubts.

In late May 1645 it was reported that the king was on his way and that the Scots commander was about to depart. The garrison, although paid with money made from the citizens' plate, was very hard-pressed, and at one point celebrated with three days supply of food and drink. This was regretted almost immediately, for within the week the garrison was forced to eat rats and dogs. Later in the month it was reported that the garrison was very weak. It took the horseflesh from the citizens, whom Tullie described as growing insolent. Everybody was in a desperately poor state of health, and when the news of the king's defeat at Naseby reached the town, it asked for peace. On 25 June the articles of surrender were agreed, and three days later the Scots marched in and took command.

The Scots remained until 1647, during which time they demolished parts of the priory and the English built the 'main guard', a form of citadel with bastions and gun ports, in the market place. They also improved the defences of the castle, using stone taken from the priory. The English returned, but a fresh Royalist rising occurred in 1648 and the city once more changed hands. By October 1648, however, it was clear that the city could not remain in the king's hands, and Cromwell received the surrender in person.

From the execution of the king in 1649 to the death of Cromwell in 1658, the north-west and Scotland were permanently on edge. Although effective opposition to the new regime had been ended, pockets of Royalist sympathizers could still be found, and the castle garrison was accordingly maintained. Thereafter, difficulties in Carlisle were fanned not so much by military as by religious considerations. In 1653 George Fox, the Quaker, had preached in the cathedral, and elsewhere in the county he attracted support from the soldiers. In 1663 plans were discovered for a more widespread rebellion against Charles II, 'a tyrant' as he was described. This rebellion fell apart, but the presence of Scottish Presbyterians who refused to compromise their principles continued to make the government nervous for many years. The garrison continued to be maintained, although it had little to do.

The castle was refurbished by Sir Christopher Musgrave, as governor, in the 1680s. Despite the revival of Catholicism with the crowning of James II in 1685, and the strategic importance of Carlisle, the castle gradually stagnated. Carlisle was largely unaffected by the events of the Glorious Revolution, and the Jacobite rebellion in 1715 bypassed the town, except insofar as rebels were incarcerated in the castle. Religious dissent was partly overcome by the establishment of a Presbyterian Church of Scotland in 1690, and as continental affairs absorbed the attention of the crown and government, Carlisle slipped off the national agenda. In the early eighteenth century the castle garrison comprised only two companies of Invalids from the Chelsea Hospital and three officers; it was merely a token presence. Even the captain of one of these companies seems to have had a fairly relaxing time painting and fishing, as 'for many years the many rivers about Carlisle turned them all into fishermen'. So decrepit had the defences become that the citizens were demolishing the walls, and in 1739 the governor was advised not to use the wall between the castle and town 'for fear it should break down'.

The leisurely pace of life in the years after the Restoration of the monarchy in 1660 was reflected in the gradual transformation of the city into the principal social centre within the county. The fairs, markets and quarter sessions attracted the gentry and merchants from many places. But to many visitors in the eighteenth century Carlisle appeared thoroughly provincial and backward. Daniel Defoe could find little to say about it, noting only that it was 'at the utmost extent of England'. Celia Fiennes, a few years earlier, was more forthcoming, but scarcely more complimentary. The cathedral, she wrote, 'looked stately but nothing curious', and she noted a few good houses, and commented on the 'broad and handsome' streets. Her general lack of enthusiasm may perhaps have been coloured by her accommodation. After the first hostelry she stayed in over-charged her, Celia Fiennes moved to the biggest house in the town. Unfortunately for her it proved to have 'the worst accommodation . . . with a young giddy landlady that could only dress fine and entertain the soldiers'. The

A stone-mullioned window, blocked up and concealed behind later plaster at 65 Scotch Street, revealed during demolition in 1981

impressions of Celia Fiennes and Daniel Defoe were confirmed by a correspondent of Hutchinson, one of Cumbria's early historians, who noted that 'Carlisle, about the beginning of the present (i.e. eighteenth) century, exhibited no marks of modern convenience of elegance. The buildings, mostly of wood clay and laths, bespoke the poverty and bad taste of the inhabitants.' Hutchinson's view was tinged with romanticism, however, and the desire to emphasize the advances Carlisle had made during that century. Clearly, we cannot always take contemporary accounts at face value.

The spread of religious nonconformism had its effect on the appearance of Carlisle and other towns. While the rural areas of Cumbria may have been deeply rooted in the Church of England, the towns, with a population including an element of non-locals, provided a haven for dissenting communities. In the eighteenth century the early dissenters, the Quakers, the Presbyterians and the Congregationalists, all of whom shared the same missionary zeal, were joined by another group aroused by the passion of one of the greatest of all evangelists, John Wesley.

Initially there were three dissenting churches in Carlisle, all of Scottish origin. Edward James, a Presbyterian, acquired a property in Blackfriars Street and it was probably here, initially in secret during the 1650s, that meetings were first held. How large the congregation was is uncertain, and it was not until 1737 that the first purpose-built Presbyterian church was established in Fisher Street. The Congregationalists held sway at their church in Annetwell Street. These were among the first new places of worship to be established in Carlisle since the reign of Henry VIII. Their congregations may have been small and their influence at this time was perhaps limited, but their very presence shows that the city was gradually changing.

The appearance of Carlisle gradually changed in other ways. Many of the buildings may well have been medieval in aspect, but there were an increasing number of houses made from brick and stone. Brick was used at Tullie House and in the Cathedral Close in the 1680–90s. At about this time many of the houses on Scotch Street were being rebuilt in brick, with red sandstone cladding on the street frontage. Doubtless the bricks were supplied by brickmakers like Matthew Wildman, described as a bricklayer, who died in 1684, John Blaylock who died in 1714, or the Railton family who were active from the 1690s to 1752, At least one brick kiln in the late seventeenth century was at Murrell Hill, and others in the eighteenth century were at the Gosling Sike, Kingstown, Botcherby and Etterby Hill.

The Old Town Hall built in 1669 and later extended

It was not just the external appearance of the buildings that changed; the internal layouts were also affected. Cellars were built, possibly for the first time in Carlisle, and the shape and arrangement of rooms, the ways in which the rooms were heated, and the position of the staircases, are reminiscent of houses belonging to the late seventeenth and early eighteenth centuries at such places as Whitehaven.

This 'Great Rebuilding', as the late W.G. Hoskins called it, took place in many county towns in the sixteenth century. In Carlisle it occurred, on a piecemeal basis, in the late seventeenth and eighteenth centuries. It was not inspired by any grand plan or as a response to a disaster, such as the Fire of London in 1666, and properties were often rebuilt within the bounds of the earlier medieval boundaries. Nevertheless, the ideas and influences for the new buildings must have come from somewhere. One possibility is that some of the ideas derived from Sir John Lowther, Member of Parliament, Fellow of the Royal Society and the man responsible for much of Whitehaven's early growth.

Some of these street frontage buildings were occupied by the merchant classes, the gentry, and lawyers, who formed a very significant proportion of the town's population in the seventeenth and eighteenth centuries. Apart from the gentry, retailers and tanners were among the wealthiest people in Carlisle, and it was these people who were able to afford such prominent street frontage properties as those on Scotch Street. Members of the leather trades, notably the tanners, glovers and shoemakers, were especially prominent. Indeed, in 1684 some 45 per cent of the guildsmen were leatherworkers of one sort or another. In the seventeenth century textile-related trades appear to have been a minority concern in Carlisle, and there were few entrepreneurs compared with elsewhere in the county, a situation that had changed dramatically by the late eighteenth century.

In 1745 the genteel life of local society was rudely interrupted when the strategic position of the city came to the fore again. In the previous year fears had been expressed about the possibility of another Jacobite uprising, and this led to an inspection of the castle cannons. It was just as well, for the inspection revealed that small boys had blocked the touch-holes with wooden plugs. The militia was raised and arms supplied, but the defences were still woefully inadequate. The city walls on the eastern side of the town were partly demolished, while parts of the castle were described as being thin and decayed. On the

View of Carlisle Castle by Samuel Buck, 1739

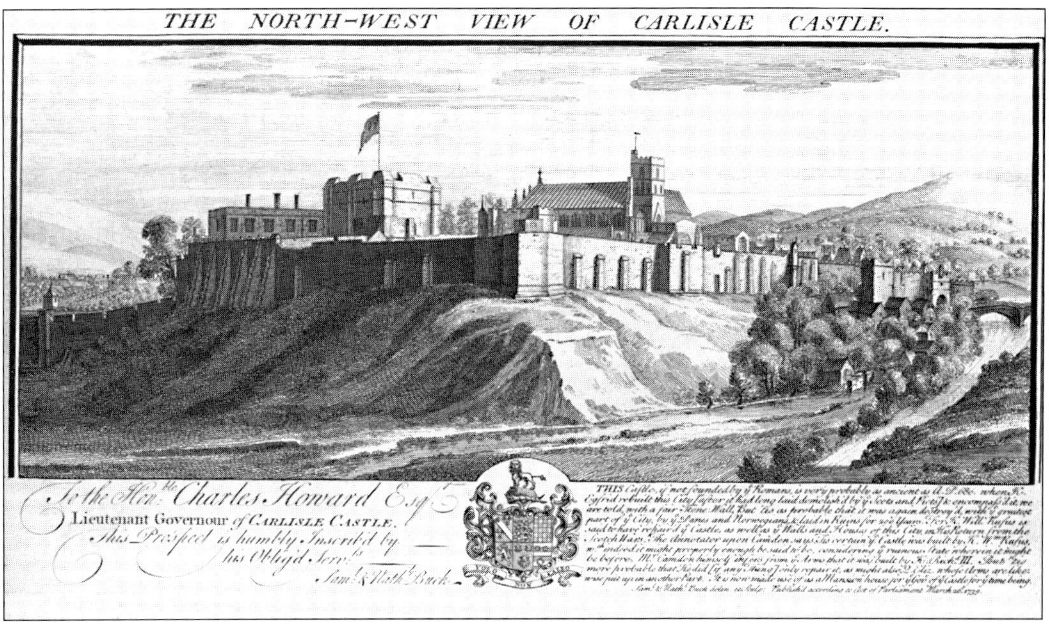

whole the people of Carlisle were not very concerned, and as late as October 1745 they seem to have thought that, as in 1715, they would never be attacked. After all, Carlisle had escaped attack for almost a hundred years. They were mistaken, for on Saturday 9 November the Jacobite army began arriving at Carlisle.

It was a somewhat ludicrous start to a siege, for as the Highlanders arrived they became mixed up with people going home from the market laden with shopping. The garrison was unable to fire on the Jacobites until the shoppers had passed by. By evening, however, the besiegers were demanding billets, and the following day Prince Charles Edward Stuart, the Young Pretender, sent in a summons to the townsfolk to surrender. This was greeted with cannon fire. Such bravado was not to last, for within a few days the militia and townsfolk were exhausted, people were deserting, and there was talk of capitulation. The commanding officer, Lieutenant Colonel James Durand, determined to hold out and made what preparations he could

Engraving by Thomas Hearne about 1777 showing the Outer Gatehouse with its wooden drawbridge and the ditch filled with water

to secure the castle, but its defences were so weak, and the garrison so poor, that he had little choice but to surrender. This took place on 15 November, and two days later the Young Pretender himself arrived. He seems to have stayed for only one night before moving south with his army. This must have been a great relief to the townsfolk who complained that the Highlanders had 'behaved in a most beastly manner'. A month later they were back, but this time in retreat. The Duke of Cumberland surrounded the city and the castle, which he described as being an 'old hen coop', and directed his fire from Stanwix and Primrose Bank.

Cumberland retook Carlisle and immediately hanged some of the Jacobites. Eventually the majority were transported to North America, but others were sent for trial. Some ninety-six prisoners were condemned to death. After the trial the prisoners were secured by 7 ft long chains attached to an iron bar fixed to a wall, probably in the keep. Those that were executed were sent to the gallows at Harraby Hill, Brampton and Penrith. In the following year the Jacobites were roundly defeated at Culloden, and Durand was court-martialled for surrendering the city. The aftermath of the siege took the same form as in previous centuries. Various plans were put forward for strengthening the defences, but the crown's priorities elsewhere effectively meant that little was done to improve them. The result was that the castle and city defences continued their decline into picturesque decay.

The Transformation of Carlisle

If Carlisle was a sleepy county town remote from the centre of power, fashion and trade in the mid-eighteenth century, it was transformed into a filthy, overcrowded, noisy industrial and commercial town a hundred years later. A population level of around 4,000–5,000 in the late eighteenth century had risen to a little under 10,000 by 1801, the year of the first census, but increased to over 35,000 by 1841. The rise in the population continued through the nineteenth century, and Carlisle was, of course, no different to many other towns experiencing similar growth. To the people of Carlisle, however, it was a matter of pride. This is evident in the works of the Carlisle-born poet, Robert Anderson (1770–1833), who lived through these early years of growth. Disillusioned with life in London, Anderson returned to Carlisle where he composed many poems celebrating what to him were the unique qualities of Carlisle and Cumberland:

Shaddon Mill, built by Peter Dixon in 1836, was one of the largest cotton mills in Britain in its heyday

But we've monie fine castles, whoar fit our brave fadders
When Cummerlan' could any country defy
We help yen anudder; we welcome the stranger;
Ourselves and our country we'll ever defend. . . .

No single factor can explain the rapid growth of Carlisle. In the mid- to late eighteenth century the production of textiles increased in importance, initiated by the woollen factory established by the Hamburg merchants, the brothers Guliker. Their business soon foundered, but by 1774 at least five manufacturers were producing textiles in Carlisle. They included the Fergusons who, besides operating in the city, also built a new cotton mill at Warwick Bridge. The Fergusons were related by marriage to another local textile entrepreneurial family, the Dixons, who built Shaddon Mill and its 320 ft high chimney in 1836. Most of the cotton mills in Carlisle were located around the Caldew, on the western side of the city centre.

During the first half of the nineteenth century Carlisle became the leading industrial and commercial centre in the county, with much of its prosperity built on service and manufacturing industries, textile production being the most important until the 1850s. Indeed, in the early nineteenth century Carlisle was considered to be the fourth most important centre of textile production in Britain, and locally accounted for over 50 per cent of the female workforce until mid-century.

But there were other growing businesses. Carlisle had long been known as a centre of clockmaking in Cumberland. Although some of the 100 or more clockmakers recorded in Carlisle were present from the late seventeenth century, the majority were in business in the later eighteenth and nineteenth centuries. The most important of these families, and by far the most prolific clockmakers, was the Blaylocks who had a hand in other businesses as well.

Other early industries included the metalwares. In 1806 Richard and William Porter leased the Carlisle Old Foundry in Blackfriars Street, on the site of the former Dominican friary. They made cast-iron goods, fire grates and other items. They were competing with two other ironfounders, Burgess & Hayton in Lowther Street and Dalston & Bell in Botchergate, but it was Porters who by 1850 had emerged as the principal ironfounder and one of the main local brickmakers, supplying the Admiralty dockyards in Chatham, among others, with bricks.

Communications was a factor of major concern at this time. In an attempt to improve transport systems between Carlisle and the Solway a canal was dug. Initially intended to link Carlisle and Maryport, Carlisle Canal never got further than what is now Port Carlisle on the Solway coast. From 1823 passengers for Liverpool, or ultimately America, were able to embark on the *Arrow* at Caldewgate and sail the 11 miles to Port Carlisle, where they transferred to larger vessels. The water levels in the canal were maintained by the largest beam engine pump in the country. The canal was eventually killed off by the railways and closed in 1853 when it was converted into the single-line Port Carlisle Railway. The pump survived, however, and was taken to Cannock Chase where it was used until the early twentieth century as a canal pumping engine.

The first railway to open in Carlisle was the western end of the Newcastle and Carlisle Railway in 1836. Two years later the line was complete, and it became the first railway across England to be opened. Large crowds witnessed the opening, with some passengers in the open trucks being drenched with heavy rain. By 1845 the Maryport to Carlisle Railway was providing the first rail link between the North Sea and the Irish Sea.

The Citadel station, first built in 1847 to the design of Sir William Tite, was one of several stations operating in the early years of the railways

Ultimately, with seven railway companies operating, Carlisle became the railway centre of the north, competing only with York in the number of companies it served. Its principal passenger station was at the Citadel, but initially it was not the only one. The first passenger station serving the Newcastle and Carlisle Railway was at London Road, built in 1835, and the Maryport and Carlisle Railway opened its own terminus at Crown Street in 1844. The Port Carlisle Railway also had its own station at Canal in 1854. Eventually this proliferation of stations was resolved and passenger activities were centred on the Citadel, where each railway company had its own booking office. The Citadel had not been designed for such a large number of trains, and the station as completed in 1850 had to be progressively enlarged.

Other transport improvements also took place. An abortive attempt to introduce horse-drawn buses in the 1830s was abandoned in 1858 because of the lack of custom. New omnibuses began operating at the end of the century, and trams began running in 1900, powered by electricity from the new Electric Lighting Station.

But it was the railways that in various ways provided some of the biggest entrepreneurial and employment opportunities in Carlisle. The arrival of rail transport stimulated the growth of many other industries. The clockmaker, John Blaylock, took the opportunities at hand. He was the founder of the Carlisle City and District Banking Company, and provided all the station clocks between Carlisle and Preston, besides making ticket machines. He collaborated with a newcomer to Carlisle, one William Pratchitt, and set up the firm of Blaylock & Pratchitt at the Long Island Ironworks in 1859. The firm was very successful, and made, among other things, much of the ironwork for a great many northern railway stations. By 1904 the firm, now Pratchitt Brothers, had been given a Royal Warrant following its work at Sandringham.

Cowans and Sheldon Engineering Works also owed its origins to this astonishing period of industrial growth. In 1846 John Cowans and Edward Sheldon, both former apprentices of Robert Stephenson, arrived in Carlisle from the north-east. They took over a small business at Woodbank and within a few years were manufacturing axles, wagon wheels and railway turntables.

Where railways were not directly responsible for growth, they assisted the development of other industries. Without the rail network to distribute his biscuits, Jonathan Dodgson Carr would have been unlikely to have enjoyed such a degree of success on a national scale. Carr arrived in Carlisle in 1831, and from humble beginnings as a baker in Castle Street he soon concentrated activities in his Steam

Biscuit Factory in Caldewgate. He must have already had a considerable local market for his biscuits, as the local population had by now exceeded 19,000, and some ten years after arriving in Carlisle he had obtained the Royal Warrant. By 1846 Carr was making some 400 tons of biscuits annually, his success due partly to the adaptation of a printing machine to one which cut biscuits; before then biscuits were cut by hand.

Hudson Scott, Carr's friend and fellow Quaker, began a printing and stationery business, but he too saw the opportunities in manufacturing. By 1876 he developed methods of transfer-printing on to tin plate, and Carr took advantage of this development for packaging biscuits. This helped build up the tin-plate manufacturing industry noted by Mrs Beeton, who observed in 1895 that 'an important trade has grown up within the last quarter of a century in tinned goods of all kinds'. In 1882 Hudson Scott was employing 200 people and the numbers grew to 370 in 1890 and with some 1,200 in 1906 the firm had emerged as one of Carlisle's principal employers. Hudson Scott was one of the forerunners of the Metal Box Company, which was formed as a result of a merger with other manufacturers in 1922.

Life in Carlisle

Carlisle at the beginning of the nineteenth century was little bigger than some five hundred years earlier, but some fifty years later it had completely altered. By the 1850s building had extended along Port Road and Newtown Road, including the hospital, which opened as the Infirmary in 1841. The land to the west of Shaddongate, now occupied by Rigg Street and Newcastle Street, was being infilled. On the eastern side of Carlisle, the broad thoroughfare of Lowther Street was built up on its eastern side, where the Athenaeum and the Congregational chapel were situated. From here led Victoria Place, Lonsdale Street and Chapel Street. The land between West Walls and the railway lines was filling up, as might be expected, while to the south along Botchergate new housing was provided in the vicinity of the Workhouse on Fusehill Street.

Nor was development confined to the land outside the former walled area. Within the city centre itself the old city walls, long since in a state of advanced decay, were gradually pulled down along East and West Tower Streets and Lowther Street, a process complete by 1815. The Lanes area in the eighteenth century probably had large areas of open land with relatively little development behind the Scotch

Street frontage, but during the nineteenth century it was rapidly infilled with a multitude of tenements, workshops and small business premises.

Much of the new housing was built by the Carlisle Building Society or the Cumberland Building Society in the early to middle years of the nineteenth century. But among the most remarkable individual initiatives was that of Laings. From small beginnings at Sebergham in 1848, James Laing moved to Carlisle and established business premises in Newcastle Street, off Shaddongate. There was much construction work to be had in Carlisle, in housing as well as in other spheres. Over 3,700 new houses were built in Carlisle between 1881 and 1903. In 1900 terraced houses were being built for £150–£175 each, and let at five to six shillings a week. By 1900 the firm had expanded to the point where new offices were required at Milbourne Street and the corner of Oswald and Linton Streets on London Road. Besides housing, Laing built the Electric Lighting Station in 1898, and around the same time secured a prime contract for building the Ashley Street schools. Private developers continued to build houses, but in the 1920s–30s the Borough Council provided the main initiative by erecting Council estates throughout the suburbs, from Belah in the north to Harraby, Raffles and Botcherby.

Life in nineteenth-century Carlisle was not easy, despite the growing employment opportunities and better transport facilities. Some employers, notably Laing, Carr and Hudson Scott, ran their businesses on religious principles, influenced first by the Quakers and later by the Brethren. Jonathan Dodgson Carr, for example, not only provided housing for his employees, but near to his works, he installed hot baths, a library and reading room. By the mid- to late nineteenth century nonconformist religious groups had proliferated, and were attracting all sections of society to their colours. This was due in no small measure to the many outstanding preachers who visited Carlisle at the behest of such evangelists as John Whitridge and his successor Thomas Woodrow (grandfather of the later President of the United States), both from their Congregational church at Annetwell Street. In the case of the Church of Scotland, however, it was less the quality of the speakers and more the arrival of the railways, with large numbers of Scots involved in the construction programme, which led to the foundation of its church on Chapel Street.

Internal disputes, very short pastorates, unordained preachers and other problems led to many leaving the original core of seventeenth-century dissenters. The Brethren owed its origin to Quakerism, J.D. Carr being one of those who left the Friends for the Brethren. At

An aerial view of The Lanes in 1980 showing the dense pattern of nineteenth-century infilling between Scotch Street (bottom) and Lowther Street (top)

the Annetwell Street Congregational church, continuing difficulties over many years in the nineteenth century ultimately led to the foundation of churches in Lowther Street, Charlotte Street and Cecil Street. At these churches railwaymen, shopkeepers and servants rubbed shoulders with the Blaylocks, the Carrs and Hudson Scotts. By the beginning of the present century, there were large numbers of chapels, churches and missions all over the city.

The employees of such enlightened men as Carr and Laing may have counted themselves as fortunate, but others were not so well placed. In 1850 the Report of the Carlisle Sanitary Association felt 'bound to express their extreme regret that Carlisle should present so much filth, and so many nuisances of the worst kind . . .'. It was noted that in Rickergate Ward, for example, 'the committee can hardly find words to express the amount of filth . . . fever (cholera) has found numerous victims in East Tower Street and Drover's Lane . . . in Moffat's Yard there is only one privy for 28 families, other properties being without conveniences at all, and in some of the lodging houses more than 20 people are living in one room, and that adjacent to the filthiest privies and dunghills'.

Generally speaking, levels of health in Carlisle were precarious in the extreme. Before the advent of proper sewerage and drainage schemes, local water supplies were almost invariably tainted. In 1850 Dr Murray, Professor of Chemistry at Edinburgh, wrote that 'the common well water in Carlisle was scarcely fit to be used by the lowest class of animals . . . no water from the pumps is fit for drinking'. As Carlisle expanded the need for water increased, and in 1909 a reservoir at Castle Carrock was finally opened to supply the town.

In the early nineteenth century, before the advent of the railways, textile production was the main source of employment. But as the century progressed, despite the increasing job opportunities, unemployment and poverty were recognized as increasing social problems. Workhouses such as the one in Fusehill Street, now the City General Hospital, were built for paupers at various times. The handloom weavers of Caldewgate, desperate at the government's attempts to hold down wages, rioted in 1819. This caused great consternation and the military was put on a state of alert in the castle, but the incident passed off relatively peacefully compared with that at

Prisoners' cells next to the Gatehouse at Carlisle Castle. The 'black hole' (to the left with the chimney) was built in 1832 and in 1840 new cells were added

The women's cells at Carlisle gaol shortly before demolition

Peterloo. The Carlisle weavers were at the forefront of the Radicalism that eventually led to the Reform Act.

With low wages, high food prices and unemployment, it is not surprising that crime flourished. In 1850 the Chief Constable reported that 'the increase in apprehension [arrests] is owing to drunkenness and want of employment', a sentiment that strikes a chord today. However, his conclusion that 'the borough is in a peaceable and orderly state' suggests that he was also something of a politician with an eye to potential criticism. Gas lighting, introduced to Carlisle in 1819, had a beneficial impact on crime rates as far as the police and the City Council were concerned. Where there was gas lighting, it was said, there was less chance of 'robbery, immorality and mischief'. Age and pressure on space in the gaol in 1821 led to the County being called to account 'for insufficiency' in respect of the County Gaol. New plans were drawn up and a new County Gaol was built next to the citadel, finally opening in 1827.

Concern about drunkenness, a perpetual problem, lay behind one of the most astonishing experiments undertaken by the government. Lloyd George, fearing uprisings in England comparable to those in Ireland, set up the Central Control Board in 1916 with the express purpose of controlling liquor in Carlisle and the outlying areas. It had three main aims: the first was 'to prevent such drinking as renders workers unfit for the National Service'; the second was 'to provide cheap and good food, so as to discourage the drinking of alcohol apart from with meals'; the third aim was 'to make the public house a less

The Apple Tree Inn, Lowther Street, an example of a State Management public house designed by Harry Redfern

unhealthy and more easily supervised place for rest and refreshment; and for social intercourse and recreation'.

The Board purchased more than a third of the 100 public houses in the city; it also bought the four breweries and numerous hotels and off-licences, and centralized the distilling of whisky. The State Management Scheme, as it was known, began as an experiment, but continued for fifty-five years until it was finally wound up by the Home Secretary, Reginald Maudling, in 1971. It is not clear to what extent this experiment was considered successful, although the provision of modernized public houses would have doubtless have improved the surroundings within which people were able to get drunk!

The city centre changed its appearance in other ways in the nineteenth century. From being a largely residential area in the eighteenth century, it became an area given over primarily to shops, businesses and cultural pursuits. The rapidly growing population and the new businesses were served by a proliferation of banks, of which the earliest known was established in 1787. George Head Head of Rickerby was one of the most successful private bankers. The new buildings, such as the Cumberland Union Banking Society of 1865 (now the Midland Bank) that took over Head's bank, or the Carlisle and Cumberland Bank (now occupied by Barclays), signalled a permanent change in the appearance of the town.

The Midland Bank, English Street, built in 1898 on the site of earlier banks including the Cumberland Union Bank and later the Carlisle and Cumberland Bank

The former grammar school built in 1889 in Lowther Street

Similar changes could be seen elsewhere. In Lowther Street the first post office (now occupied by The Post public house) was built in 1863. The County Hotel, built by Anthony Salvin, the Central Plaza Hotel and the Viaduct Hotel, among others, were built to provide overnight stops for businessmen travelling by train. Small family businesses, such as Watts Coffee Shop or Sproats Boot and Clog Makers, sprang up in the nineteenth century and lasted for decades. Pre-eminent among these smaller businesses was that of Charles Thurnam, who started as a printer and bookseller in his English Street premises in 1816. Thurnam expanded to include a substantial circulating library and a pianoforte business, but its main work was in supplying stationery and in printing and publishing. Businesses such as Thurnam's were, in their way, as crucial to the development of Carlisle as a commercial and business centre as the banks and hotels. Without such services lubricating the wheels of commerce, many of the achievements would not have been possible.

New places of worship also contributed to the changing appearance of the city, including, in 1830, Thomas Rickman's neo-Gothic

Holy Trinity church at the junction of Port Road and Wigton Road, designed by the eminent Victorian architect Thomas Rickman

The United Reformed church in Fisher Street, built in 1894–5 by the architect T. Taylor Scott, is on the site of a succession of nonconformist churches dating back to 1731 when the Presbyterians acquired the site

churches at Holy Trinity, Caldewgate and Christchurch, Botchergate. The outstanding local architect, C.J. Ferguson, who spent time in Sir Gilbert Scott's practice in London, was involved in many local schemes including the Bush Hotel and St Aidan's Church. The cathedral had its fair share of changes. One of the country's leading cathedral architects, Ewan Christian, was substantially responsible for the outward appearance of the cathedral church in the 1850s, while shortly afterwards a dispute broke out between the Ferguson brothers and G.E. Street over the restoration of the Fratry, a dispute which reached the national press.

Cultural pursuits also marked Carlisle out as a regional centre of some importance. Doubtless Robert Burns, on his visit to the city, may not have recognized it as such, but Sir Walter Scott, who married in the cathedral and based some of his novels in Carlisle, probably did. Reading rooms sprang up in several places from the early eighteenth century, and a Mechanics Institute opened in 1824, gradually acquiring a substantial library. It was in these places that the ordinary people of Carlisle could read the news in such papers as the *Carlisle Patriot*, which was founded in 1815 and which eventually became the *Cumberland News*.

Built in 1863, The Post public house in Lowther Street was originally Carlisle's first post office. It was replaced in 1916 with the opening of larger premises on Warwick Road

A theatre was built in 1813, but a combination of opposition from religious groups and mishaps dogged it until Her Majesty's Theatre was built in Lowther Street in 1874, and later rebuilt after a fire in 1905. The Academy of Art at Finkle Street attracted outstanding local painters such as Sam Bough and Matthew Nutter. Eventually this

Formerly the Victoria Hall, Lowther Street, this purpose-built theatre was built in 1874 and later renamed Her Majesty's Theatre

became Carlisle Museum, but then the Ferguson brothers came to the rescue of the old Tullie House. In 1893, with a substantial financial contribution from their own pockets, they converted the former Tullie House into a museum and library at a cost of £20,000.

In the twentieth century further changes to the appearance of the city centre have taken place. Among the State Management Scheme's objectives was the replacement of many of the older public houses for newer, more comfortable and up-to-date premises. Harry Redfern, the architect, was employed to tear down public houses and replace them with his own distinctive designs. Some of these included The Apple Tree in Lowther Street, the Malt Shovel in Rickergate and The Crescent. The castle lost its married quarters and was eventually severed from the city with the construction of a ring-road which opened in 1974. A fundamental break with the past took place in 1977 when the City Council decided to replace many of the old vennels, lanes and most of the buildings between Scotch Street and Lowther Street with a new shopping centre. Lanes which originated in the Middle Ages, premises occupied by the Carlisle gentry in the early eighteenth century, and tenements formerly overcrowded with dozens of families cooped up together in unsanitary conditions in the nineteenth century, were demolished in the early 1980s and replaced with brand new shops. This development, while undoubtedly benefiting the city, also physically erased a pattern of streets and lanes and thereby removed an important thread of continuity. Latterly, the construction of out-of-town shopping facilities and motorways has reduced dependence on the city centre.

In many respects the history of Carlisle compares well with many other towns. First innovation, then stability, and, finally, rapid change in the last two centuries have characterized it. What marks Carlisle out as different from many other places is its geographical isolation and its frontier position. The people of Carlisle have always identified closely with their city and its surroundings. Perhaps its remoteness and its border location are partly responsible for the conservative element in local society, but that element is deeply rooted in history. As one writer put it, 'Cumbrians, when border warfare was over and moss-trooping days had passed away, still felt that they were not as other men are.'

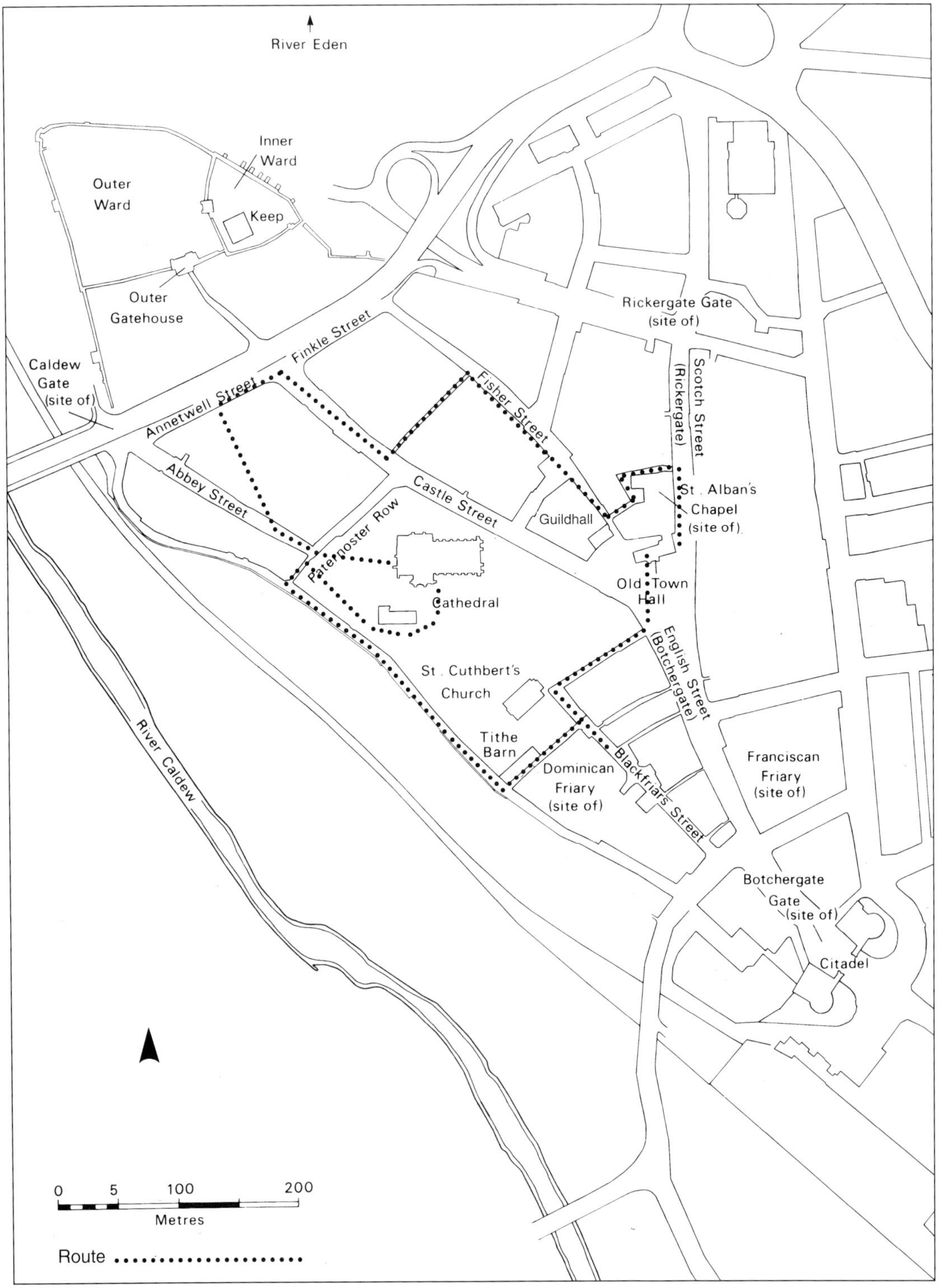
River Eden
Inner Ward
Outer Ward
Keep
Outer Gatehouse
Caldew Gate (site of)
Finkle Street
Annetwell Street
Abbey Street
Castle Street
Fisher Street
Paternoster Row
Guildhall
Rickergate Gate (site of)
Scotch Street
(Rickergate)
St. Alban's Chapel (site of)
Old Town Hall
Cathedral
St. Cuthbert's Church
Tithe Barn
English Street (Botchergate)
Dominican Friary (site of)
Blackfriars Street
Franciscan Friary (site of)
Botchergate Gate (site of)
Citadel
River Caldew
0 5 100 200
Metres
Route

A Walk Around the City Centre

This walk explores some of the streets and buildings of the ancient city centre, beginning and ending at the Old Town Hall. The walk can be extended to take in the castle and the cathedral precinct. Wheelchair users should have no difficulty with any part of the route.

Throughout this tour directions are given in bold type, and are interspersed with descriptions of the features along the route.

Visitors should meet in the Old Town Hall on the first floor (Tourist Information Centre). Here you will find an orientation display and audio-visual facilities which will help you in your tour and in planning your stay in Carlisle. There is a clearly marked lift for disabled visitors just inside the door to the right of the right-hand steps as you face the Old Town Hall.

When you come out of the Old Town Hall, you will see that you are in a large open area where four main streets converge. Standing with your back to the Old Town Hall you will face English Street. To your right and just behind you is Castle Street and Fisher Street. To your left is Scotch Street.

The pattern of streets as you now see it is ancient. It is not known when English Street was first laid out, but its alignment probably dates to the early Middle Ages. The line of English Street was partly determined by the presence of the south gate (Botchard's Gate), the site of which is below the road between the two large circular towers near the railway station, and which led down the A6 to Penrith and the Lake District. Castle Street and Fisher Street are also creations of the Middle Ages. Castle Street leads directly to the main gate of the castle, but the origin of Fisher Street is not certain. Scotch Street, however, is almost certainly Roman in origin, and led straight towards the crossing of the River Eden and thence to Scotland.

The Old Town Hall near Carlisle Cross (left)

In front of you is the Market Cross, erected in 1682, and a large open space used occasionally for open-air events such as the Great Fair. In Roman times this space also formed the intersection of several major roads, but some of these are not traceable in the streets and lanes visible today. From the Middle Ages until 1927 an open-air market was held here on Wednesdays and Saturdays. Vegetables were sold in the Greenmarket, the name given to the space in front of the Guildhall, to your right and behind you. There were permanent stalls, or shambles, used for selling meat and fish, in front of Binns store. This area has now been cleared but one of the buildings here was formerly the Main Guard, a defensive building erected in the Civil War. Binns and Marks and Spencer are on the site of Highmoor House, where both Bonnie Prince Charlie and the Duke of Cumberland stayed during the 1745 Jacobite Rebellion.

Before starting the tour it is worth turning round and looking at the Guildhall and the Old Town Hall itself. The Guildhall is the only example in Carlisle of a medieval half-timbered building. Now a museum, and open to visitors in the summer, it was built in the mid-fourteenth century as a private house and rebuilt by a London merchant, Richard of Redness, at the turn of the fourteenth and fifteenth centuries. It was acquired by the Corporation, and from the sixteenth century it was used as the Guildhall and provided rooms for the main guilds to meet in, including the Merchants, Tanners, Skinners and Glovers, Tailors, Weavers, Smiths, Shoemakers and Butchers.

The Old Town Hall dates to 1669, and was extended in 1717. A Town Hall, or Moot Hall, has stood on this site for centuries.

Now walk to your right in the direction of Binns and go down St Cuthbert's Lane. There is an attractive group of small shops on the right, and at the end you will see St Cuthbert's Parish Church; to your left is Blackfriars Street.

St Cuthbert's Lane is an ancient thoroughfare, and building work in the nineteenth century revealed fragments of Anglo-Saxon sculpture, doubtless originating from the monastery established hereabouts by St Cuthbert in AD 685. The church is worth looking at inside, especially for its galleries. The present building dates to 1788, but a church is known to have stood here from the early Middle Ages. One unusual feature is that the church is not aligned east–west as are most Christian churches, and this may be due to the presence of much earlier Roman buildings.

Walk down Blackfriars Street and stop under the Marks and Spencer bridge.

The rear of Binns store, to your left, is the site of Carlisle's first purpose-built theatre, McCready's Theatre, built in 1813. Blackfriars Street is a Roman street in origin, and in 1977 archaeological excavations where the Marks and Spencer Food Hall now stands revealed part of the Roman road and buildings along its frontage. In the Middle Ages the Food Hall was the site of the Dominican or Blackfriars friary. The entrance lay next to the eighteenth-century Sportsman public house.

Retrace your steps and turn left down Heads Lane. At the end you will emerge on to West Walls. From this point you have a fine view across the western side of Carlisle.

West Walls is a narrow, winding road along the city walls on the western side of the ancient city. Looking over the parapet you will see how the land drops away to the railways in front, and just beyond, although partly hidden today, is the fast flowing River Caldew. The Caldew provided the power for numerous mills in the eighteenth century, while various leats or mill-races were also built for additional water power. The most prominent building on the skyline is Shaddon Mill, with its 300 ft high chimney. Shaddon Mill was built in 1836 by Peter Dixon, one of the leading cotton manufacturers of his day. Further to the right can be seen the kiln for a former brewery standing on the bank of the River Caldew, while in the distance is United Biscuits, formerly Carr's Biscuits, one of the country's leading biscuit makers since the 1830s. It was from around there that Robert Bruce launched his attacks on the city in 1315, and became bogged down in the quagmires created by the bad weather and his soldiers.

Turn round and you will see the medieval Tithe Barn on the corner of Heads Lane and West Walls. The Tithe Barn is normally open to visitors.

The Tithe Barn dates from the fifteenth century. The massive medieval timbers form an impressive eight-bay structure that may have been built by Prior Gondibour after the siege of Carlisle in 1461.

West Walls looking north from near the fifteenth-century Tithe Barn. The former grammar-school buildings are on the right while beyond are the much repaired precinct walls of the priory

It was here that the tithes, or rents in kind, due to the cathedral canons were collected.

When you come out of the Tithe Barn back on to West Walls, disabled visitors should turn right and proceed until Dean Tait's Lane is reached. On your right are the red sandstone walls of the cathedral buildings.

For the able-bodied visitor it is worth turning left for a few yards and then going down the steps below West Walls towards the car parks. From here you will get a fine view of the city walls. At the bottom of the steps you will see the blocked up Sallyport, a small medieval gateway through the walls. At the bottom of the steps continue straight ahead parallel with the city walls until you come to another flight of steps that leads back up on to West Walls at the end of Dean Tait's Lane.

Go up the lane and under the archway, turning right through another archway into the cathedral precinct.

The City Walls, or West Walls, most clearly seen from the car parks below, have stood here since the twelfth century. Like all buildings they will have needed constant repairs and maintenance and the stonework visible today is a hotch-potch of periods.

The cathedral gatehouse is at the end of Dean Tait's Lane and at the corner of Paternoster Row and Abbey Street. It is known as Prior Slee's Gate, after the prior responsible for building it in 1528. The great wooden doors are original.

The cathedral was founded as an Augustinian priory in 1123 by King Henry I, and ten years later he created the Diocese of Carlisle. The priory served several purposes: it was a house of Augustinian canons, the mother church of the diocese and the parish church of St Mary. After Henry VIII dissolved the monasteries in the 1530s, many abbeys and priories fell into ruin, but the priory at Carlisle survived because it fulfilled a diocesan and parochial function. In its original state the priory would have resembled other monastic institutions, with a church and a series of buildings arranged round a cloister. This is not so easy to envisage today at Carlisle because some of the buildings have long since been demolished.

Walk towards the cathedral church from the gatehouse.

Prior Slee's gatehouse at the cathedral seen from Abbey Street built in 1527

On your left is number 2, The Abbey, a fine seventeenth-century house built in sandstone and extended in handmade brick. The house is now linked to the gatehouse at one end, but the other end is adjacent to a graveyard at the west end of the cathedral. The graveyard, on the site of the cathedral nave, is slightly higher than the footpath. The nave, because of its poor condition, was largely demolished at the end of the Civil War, but the position of the piers can be seen from the two incorporated into buttresses. Archaeological excavations took place here in 1989 and revealed the cathedral's Norman foundations and a Viking-age cemetery underneath. Some of the finds from the excavation, together with the church foundations, can be seen in the Treasury, an underground museum entered through the cathedral.

On your right is the Fratry, formerly the refectory of the priory in the Middle Ages. The Fratry originally formed the southern side of the cloister with the church on the northern side. Nothing now remains of the west range of the cloister, but its position is clearly seen in the footpath and herb garden leading to the Fratry door, and the footpath and tulip tree planted by the Queen in 1991. Below the Fratry is a fine medieval undercroft with a vaulted ceiling where refreshments can be obtained. Disabled visitors may have difficulty getting down the steps into the undercroft.

On the left is the cathedral church. At the west end the grey blocks of sandstone are part of the original Norman church, but much of the red sandstone is later. The fine door into the cathedral is the work of the distinguished Victorian church architect, Ewan Christian, while the choir and east end are medieval in date. Opposite the south door are the ruins of an arch and medieval walls. This is the east range of the cloister. The arch is part of the doorway into the octagonal chapter house, the site of which is partly under the footpath and the adjacent garden. The medieval walls next to the chapter house door are the remains of a vaulted undercroft below the dormitory.

The glories of the cathedral church, especially the fine east window, recently restored, are best appreciated from the inside, where guides are always available to show visitors round.

Walk past the cathedral towards the wrought-iron Lorimer Gate. Turn right.

There are fine late seventeenth-century canonry houses, numbers 1, 3 and 6, and a splendid copper beech to either side. To the left is a large detached Victorian house, number 4, The Abbey, built by Ewan Christian in 1863.

Follow the footpath to the right and walk back behind the Fratry.

In the Middle Ages much of this area, now occupied by open space, would have been occupied by kitchens, the infirmary and other lesser buildings. On the left are single-storeyed sandstone buildings with the initials T.G. (Thomas Gondibour) over the door. These buildings, now in use as a residence, were formerly stables. Seventeenth-century buildings can be seen next to the Prior's Tower at the east end of the Deanery. The Tower, with its magnificent early sixteenth-century painted ceiling – one of the finest in northern England – is well worth visiting for those able to negotiate the narrow stairs. Visitors should ask the vergers about access.

Beyond the Victorian wing of the Deanery is a walled garden, the site of further medieval buildings. Next is Bishop Smith's Registry, originally a library, where the date 1699 can be seen over the door.

Go through Prior Slee's Gate.

On the right is Paternoster Row, with a mixture of eighteenth- and nineteenth-century buildings overlooking the cathedral churchyard. Some of these buildings have recently been acquired by the new University of Northumbria.

Walk down Abbey Street and turn right through wrought-iron gates into the grounds of Tullie House.

Abbey Street contains a pleasing mix of buildings dating from the seventeenth to the twentieth centuries. In the spring and

Tullie House built by Thomas Tullie in 1689 on the site of White Hall in Abbey Street

summer the gardens of Tullie House offer a quiet and peaceful respite to the busy life of the town centre. Tullie House is now a fine museum and art gallery, but the original building was erected in 1689 by Thomas Tullie, Dean of Carlisle Cathedral. The house and gardens also lie on top of what is believed to be the forum of the Roman town. Massive Roman foundations were observed during a programme of sewer renewal in Abbey Street some years ago, and the so-called 'shrine' in the gardens may be part of the forum complex.

Walk through the gardens turning first left and then right. Enter the museum either up the steps or via the ramp for the disabled. Visitors can walk through the ground floor of the museum and visit the shop and restaurant, but there is a charge for access to the galleries. Go through the main doors and you will face Carlisle Castle.

To the left, on Annetwell Street, are new studios occupied by Radio Cumbria. The studios and much of the new part of Tullie House occupy the site of the Roman fort. Here were discovered the spectacularly well-preserved remains of the fort defences, including the south gate, and internal buildings such as barracks. The site of the fort continues across the ring-road and is under the grassed area in front of the castle.

The castle is one of the glories of Carlisle. As you face the castle, stone walls can be seen projecting towards the ring-road to the left and right. These are the city walls that, by linking the castle with the city, formed a continuous barrier and rendered the task of attack much more difficult. The point at which the ring-road cuts across the line of the walls to the left is the site of the Irish Gate, the medieval gate leading out of the city to the coast.

In front you can see the massive sandstone walls of the outer bailey and the impressive outer gatehouse (De Ireby's Tower), which has been the main entrance to the castle from the twelfth century. Behind the walls can be seen the keep, while in the corner to the far right, behind the relatively fresh red sandstone, was the site of Queen Mary's Tower. Here Mary Queen of Scots was incarcerated for a short time in 1568. It was this tower that inspired the artist J.M.W. Turner to produce a pen-and-ink drawing in 1797.

Access to the castle can be obtained by way of an underpass below the ring-road. A tour is thoroughly recommended, but disabled visitors should note that some parts are accessible up narrow stairs only on foot. Turn right and go down Castle Street.

Castle Street may have been laid out on its present alignment in the twelfth or thirteenth centuries, and clearly formed the main road to the castle gate. On the right-hand side is the fine red sandstone building that originally formed the entrance to the Tullie House Museum as extended in 1893. On the left is Long Lane, a narrow lane now linking Castle Street with Fisher Street. This is an ancient right of way now bounded by high walls, but at one time there were buildings on either side.

Go down Long Lane.

At the end of Long Lane you will emerge on to Fisher Street. The origin of this road is uncertain, but there is a suggestion that it was laid out very early after the Norman arrival and provided access to the original gate in the castle at its south-east corner.

Turn right and go up Fisher Street past the entrance to the Market Hall on the left.

The covered market was completed in 1889 and opened with great pomp and ceremony. The market replaced the earlier Butcher Market which had, until the late eighteenth century, been located near the front of the Old Town Hall. Market Street, on the left, was laid out in the late nineteenth century, while St Mary's Gate on the right is a twentieth-century creation. Beyond the market entrance is an archway to Treasury Court, another modern feature which, with its outdoor restaurant and coffee facilities in the summer, provides a welcome respite. Further up Fisher Street, near the Greenmarket, lived goldsmiths in medieval times, and it may be near here that the mint was located in the twelfth and thirteenth centuries.

Go past Treasury Court and turn left by the Kings Head public house down Rosemary Lane.

Rosemary Lane follows a 'dog-leg' course. It is an ancient route between Fisher Street and Scotch Street, and skirts the graveyard (now built over) of the medieval church of St Alban.

At the end of Rosemary Lane turn right and walk up Scotch Street back towards the Old Town Hall.

There has been a road on the line of Scotch Street since Roman times. At the bottom end of the street the land falls away near the tower block (the Civic Centre) to the River Eden. On the left-hand side of Scotch Street, walking towards the Old Town Hall, is the modern Lanes development. In 1982 some 5 acres of the city centre were demolished after twenty-five years of uncertainty, and a new shopping development was erected. The present street frontage of the Lanes was designed to maintain the scale and general appearance of the buildings that were demolished.

The Lanes area was on the eastern edge of the Roman settlement and the medieval town. Very extensive archaeological excavations took place here from 1978 to 1982, uncovering many Roman and medieval buildings and a vast array of artefacts. A detailed record of the buildings was made prior to demolition. One of those demolished was the house of Margery Jackson, the well-known Carlisle miser who died in 1814 at the age of ninety. Margery Jackson was simply one of many prominent local people who had homes on Scotch Street in the vicinity of the Market Square.

On the right-hand side is another new shopping mall known as St Alban's Walk. On this site lay the medieval church dedicated to St Alban. This, in turn, occupies the site of a Roman town-house, complete with central heating system, that was still in use in the fifth century AD.

This completes our tour of the city centre, but it does not exhaust the possibilities. Apart from Carlisle Castle, which presents difficulties of access to the disabled visitor, and the cathedral, visitors can walk through The Lanes to Lowther Street, the site of the former city walls on the eastern side. Lowther Street contains a number of buildings of interest, including The Post public house, which was the first post

The site of the medieval church and later chantry chapel dedicated to St Alban lies below the modern buildings (centre) on Scotch Street

office in Carlisle, and the Congregational church where there is a plaque recording the association of Woodrow Wilson, President of the United States, with his ancestor, Thomas Woodrow, pastor in Carlisle in the 1820s.

The Next Steps

Tullie House Museum and Art Gallery, open daily except Christmas Day and New Year's Day. Admission charge.

The Guildhall Museum, open daily April to September. Admission charge.

The Border Regiment Museum, Carlisle Castle, open daily except Christmas Day, Boxing Day, New Year's Eve and New Year's Day. Admission charge.

Carlisle Castle (English Heritage), open daily except Christmas Day and New Year's Day. Admission charge.

Carlisle Cathedral Treasury, open daily. Free.

Carlisle Cathedal Prior's Tower ceiling, open by appointment with the Verger.

There is no comprehensive history of either Carlisle in Roman times or in the Dark Ages. Readers are referred to archaeological reports, such as the two below, and to magazines such as *Current Archaeology*, which contain short accounts of recent discoveries. Summerson's *History* of the medieval city is a very thorough analysis of the major written sources, while the work on *Carlisle Castle* by McCarthy, Summerson and Annis is one of the most detailed accounts of any castle in Britain. Perriam's illustrated history is an extremely useful guide, especially for the modern periods that have not otherwise been comprehensively surveyed. For the recent history of Carlisle there are many accounts of the railways, of which that by Robinson is one of the most authoritative. Individual topics are often covered in the *Transactions of the Cumberland and Westmorland Antiquarian and Archaeological Society*.

Most of the books cited here can be easily obtained either in the Tourist Information Centre, The Cathedral Bookshop, The Castle, the bookshop in Tullie House Museum and bookshops in the city centre.

Carlisle Cathedral, A Pitkin Guide, 1991.

Carlisle The Border City, A Pitkin Guide, 1992.

McCarthy, M.R., Summerson, H.R.T., and Annis, R.G., *Carlisle Castle: A survey and documentary history*, English Heritage,

Historic Buildings and Monuments Commission Archaeological Report No 18, London, 1990.

McCarthy, M.R., *A Roman, Anglian and Medieval site at Blackfriars Street, Carlisle: Excavations 1977–9*, Kendal, 1990.

McCarthy, M.R., *Roman Waterlogged Remains at Castle Street, Carlisle: Excavations 1981–2*, Kendal, 1991.

Perriam, D.R., *Carlisle: an illustrated history*, Carlisle, 1992.

Platt, Colin and McCarthy, Mike, *Carlisle Castle, an illustrated souvenir guide*, English Heritage, London, 1992.

Robinson, P. *Rail Centres: Carlisle*, Ian Allan, London, 1986.

Summerson, H.R.T., *Medieval Carlisle: The City and the Border from the late Eleventh to the mid-Sixteenth Centuries*, forthcoming 1993.

Acknowledgements and Picture Credits

I am grateful to Denis Perriam and my wife, Catherine Brooks, for reading through the typescript and making a number of improvements. The Index is largely the work of Catherine Brooks. Carol Donnelly, Visitor Information Officer in the Tourist Information Office, kindly advised on aspects of the Walking Tour.

The line drawings are the work of Philip Cracknell, Patricia Moore and Sue Winterbottom.

The photographs on the following pages are credited to Carlisle Archaeological Unit: 2, 5, 6, 7, 9, 12, 15, 16, 17, 19, 21, 22, 24 (tombstone), 25, 29 (Birdoswald), 32, 35, 36, 44, 45, 50, 53, 57, 62, 65, 69, 73, 76, 79, 81, 85, 86, 90, 91, 92, 93, 94, 95, 96, 97, 98, 102, 104, 106, 108, 112; The Royal Commission on Historical Monuments, 24; Tullie House Museum and Art Gallery, 29; the Dean and Chapter, Carlisle Cathedral, 39, 50; Cumbria Record Office, 58; the British Library, 72; S. Stallibrass, 20; Cumbria County Library, 46, 68, 82, 83.

Index